A PRINCE AMONG STONES

A PRINCE AMONG STONES

THAT BUSINESS WITH THE ROLLING STONES AND OTHER ADVENTURES

PRINCE RUPERT LOEWENSTEIN

BLOOMSBURY

NEW YORK • LONDON • NEW DELHI • SYDNEY

Published by Bloomsbury USA, New York

All papers used by Bloomsbury USA are natural, recyclable products made from wood
grown in well-managed forests. The manufacturing processes conform to the
environmental regulations of the country of origin.

LIBRARY OF CONGRESS CATALOGING-IN-PUBLICATION DATA HAS BEEN APPLIED FOR.

ISBN: 978-1-62040-034-0

First U.S. Edition 2013

1 3 5 7 9 10 8 6 4 2

Typeset by Hewer Text UK Ltd, Edinburgh
Printed in the United States by Thompson-Shore, Inc. Dexter, Michigan

To my wife

Contents

Introduction

On 2 July 1969, a Wednesday evening, my wife and I gave a ball in the garden of our house in Holland Park. We had never thrown such a large party before: 500 guests, two live bands, one very large marquee. My wife was keen to have a theme for the night, and we decided that white should be the leitmotiv.

The décor for what we had dubbed the White Ball was conceived by David Mlinaric: splendid white floral displays, swathes of pure white drapery. Guests were expected – though not obliged – to arrive dressed all in white. My own outfit was a white suit, shirt and black bow tie, and white patent leather shoes, with, for flourish, a pair of gold buckles. My wife was 'glamorously understated' in a lace trouser suit. Only one guest bucked the trend. Marianne Faithfull arrived with Mick Jagger wearing a black gipsy dress and headscarf, and not only got away with it but drew all eyes. Mick was wearing what I can only describe as a rustic smock – which, to give him his due, *was* white. He looked like a cross between a milkmaid and one of the Evzones, the soldiers who guard the Tomb of the Unknown Soldier in Athens.

The guest list was, now I look back at it, extremely varied. At the time most balls were held in great English houses in London or the country, or perhaps Claridge's or the Hyde

Park Hotel. The hosts would invite other suitable English families and maybe a handful of friends from abroad. At our White Ball, nearly a third of the friends we had invited were from overseas, a polyglot mélange of European grandees mingled with local British society, young and old. Lady Cochrane, née Sursock (a prominent family in the Lebanon), had asked us to invite her son and newly wed daughter-in-law with an inspired sales pitch. 'They're very small and they don't drink,' she told us. We took them; both facts were true.

The black-and-white photographs that we still have in a white leather-bound album are a snapshot in time of a group of people whose lives afterwards took many unexpected turns. Arnaud de Rosnay, deep in conversation with the model and actress Marisa Berenson, was an aristocratic French playboy, who later married Isabel Goldsmith; he became a pioneer of windsurfing and disappeared in 1984 attempting to cross the Straits of Formosa. The interior designer Diana Phipps, née Sternberg, was an emigrée Czech aristocrat, who helped the future President Václav Havel while he was in prison and later returned to Bohemia to restore one of the family castles which the Havel government had handed back to her. And at a table with John Betjeman's daughter, Candida, Lord Milford Haven and Diane Halfin (who married Prince Egon von Fürstenberg a fortnight later) is Sunny von Bülow, whom we had introduced to her husband Claus two or three years earlier.

Actors and film producers mingled with the old upper class, writers and photographers with businessmen. The photographs show Cecil Beaton and the Duchess of Devonshire, Princess Margaret and Graham Mattison, an American lawyer, stockbroker and business adviser to Barbara Hutton, a man who, as I recall, was *infallibly* wrong in all his market suggestions. The film producer Sam Spiegel was there, and Peter Sellers, in a long wig and sporting a CND symbol, with Miranda Quarry, the Australian model who became his second wife the following year and is now Lady Stockton.

I had first met Mick Jagger towards the end of 1968, through an introduction by the art dealer Christopher Gibbs. Christopher, who knew the Rolling Stones well and had had them to stay at a house he was renting in Morocco, approached me to see if I would consider taking care of the finances of Mick and the rest of the Rolling Stones. The name of the group meant virtually nothing to me at the time, but I asked my wife to tell me about them. She gave me a briefing and my curiosity was tickled, and so Mick and I had seen each other frequently during the early part of 1969 before the White Ball that July.

We were very lucky that evening. There was no rain, nor was it too hot. Through Mick's connections we had music from the Skatalites and Yes, who were just about to release their first album. The ball lasted well into the early morning, continuing after Josephine and I had gone to bed. My daughter Dora's nanny later told us that the final guests had headed out on to Holland Villas Road at six o'clock. 'Who were they?' we asked. 'They were wearing white,' she reported confidently.

This party, oddly enough, marked the beginning of a new chapter in my working life. At the time, had I been asked I would have imagined that in my role as the managing director of the merchant bank Leopold Joseph my immediate future would have entailed increasing the value of the bank and providing a platform from which we could, eventually, sell it. Life is, perhaps happily, never so predictable.

The same night as the party Brian Jones was found dead at his house in Sussex. Three days later the Rolling Stones performed a most impressive memorial concert in his honour in Hyde Park, in front of nearly a quarter of a million people. Mick wore his milkmaid's dress again, and read some moving verses from Shelley's *Adonaïs*. The effect was almost like the Nuremberg Rallies.

The crowds, I thought, could definitely have started pulling down the Dorchester Hotel on Park Lane if they had felt moved to do so. I sat on the main stand and chatted to Mick before they played, not about his and the band's finances, which I was about to start reviewing, but of general matters. I asked him whether he thought that he could move the crowd into action by his voice in the way that Hitler had done. He thought carefully and replied, 'Yes. To get the crowd to pull something down would probably take twenty minutes, but to get them to build something could be done but would take much longer, say an hour.'

Things were changing, and not just in the fortunes of the Rolling Stones. The course of my own life was certainly never the same again.

1

'Only children know what they are looking for'

Antoine de Saint-Exupéry, *Le Petit Prince*

When I was fourteen, at boarding school shortly after the end of the Second World War, one of my classmates came across a comment in the social column of a paper talking about my parents getting a divorce. This was complete news to me. I had no inkling whatsoever that they were planning to do something quite so irreversible – and when I heard I was much disturbed. I went straight down to the school office and asked if I could place a reverse-charge telephone call to my mother.

I got through, and asked her, 'What's happened?' 'Darling,' she replied, 'I wasn't going to tell you, because it doesn't count.' It was her own odd interpretation of what it meant in the eyes of the Church: in her mind she had married my father and that was that. For her this divorce was purely a civil arrangement that in no way altered the fact of her marriage.

What was strange was that I had not realised that my parents had split up long before, when I was very young, maybe four or five. They lived in separate places, and indeed separate countries, my father principally in England, my mother mainly in France, but periodically they were together, and whenever I was with them both they seemed to get on very well. They certainly never spoke critically of each other.

On one occasion, puzzled by our living arrangements, I had gone so far as to question my mother, with whom I lived, on the reason all three of us did not live in the same house. 'Well, it's very easy to understand,' she said, explaining, quite plausibly, that 'Papa likes to get up early. And I like lying in bed and getting up in time for lunch. So it's really much more convenient this way.'

And so it was. I would see my father on and off (more off than on). From time to time I would go and have lunch or dinner with him where he lived just off the King's Road in Chelsea, or occasionally stay for a night or two. Whenever I saw him, there was always some nice young woman there, too, but I have few memories of any of them as they were usually never there again the next time I visited.

But I do remember staying with him when I was ten or twelve and he was living with the actress Googie Withers. Born in Karachi to a Dutch-German mother and a father who was a Royal Navy officer, she had been given the nickname Googie by her ayah: it meant 'little pigeon'. I much enjoyed meeting her, because I was fascinated by her being a film star and having seen a number of her films: she had become famous during the previous few years, appearing in *The Lady Vanishes* and *One of Our Aircraft Is Missing*. She was charming, pretty and also particularly kind to me.

There was one Easter holiday a couple of years later when my mother was in New York and my father told me he couldn't have me to stay, because, he said, it was complicated for breakfast. That I really thought was carrying things too far, although I didn't much mind. I made great friends with him in my teens, and we got on very well. Although he was distant, he was extremely witty and perceptive.

On the rare occasions I found myself alone with my father, he would talk to me about our background and our family tree, which interested me very much. I think it was the only thing my father ever talked about. From an early age he made me aware that I came from a certain sort of distinguished background.

He was Prince Leopold zu Loewenstein-Wertheim-Freudenberg, from a family that can trace itself back to Luitpold Markgrave of Carinthia and later Duke of Bavaria (who died repelling the Huns in 907).

My family is a branch of the Bavarian royal house, which started its own independent history at the end of the fifteenth century as a result of the morganatic marriage of Frederick I the Victorious, Elector Palatine, and Klara Tott, a pretty lady-in-waiting at the Palatine court. Their son, Ludwig of Bavaria, was created Sovereign Count of Loewenstein-Scharffeneck by the Holy Roman Emperor Maximilian I in 1494. His descendants made some good marriages and were then created counts of further territories.

The elder line became Protestant, thinking that their fortunes would prosper by backing Luther, whereas the younger line stayed Catholic, the family dividing in 1611 shortly before the start of the Thirty Years War. The younger line had backed the right horse and were made princes of the Holy Roman Empire in 1711, whereas my line had to wait to be made princes by the Bavarian King in 1812 after the dissolution of the Holy Roman Empire as a result of the Napoleonic

Wars in 1806 (for a fuller history and genealogy, see the Appendix, page 239).

As far as history was concerned, my father considered himself, as he later wrote, 'a mere amateur with a certain insight into our motives. What had always fascinated me about my own family was not its role in history – important up to the end of the fifteenth century, but negligible since – but the occasional flashes of eccentricity and genius which down the centuries light up and mellow those stern unvarying features of the family face.' His first conscious memory of his younger brother, for example, had been seeing him sitting on his pot aged three or four, wearing a long red dressing gown, shouting, 'One day I'll be Emperor and kill you all!'

There had been many family twists and turns, and all of those stories were fascinating to me, but my father also talked about what he called *tenue*, a single French word that has no English equivalent able to convey so successfully that blend of emotional control, impeccable manners, elegant dress and correct posture. *Tenue* was my father's touchstone.

In his late sixties, he was interviewed by the *Guardian*'s Terry Coleman, a conversation in which he talked about *tenue*, a concept in which he had been drilled by my grandfather. 'One must remain undismayed, and never show weakness.' Terry Coleman asked him whether it was anything like the English stiff upper lip. 'More than that,' my father answered, 'a stoic attitude. The attitude of the samurai in the face of death.'

Our conversations took place in his sitting room, which contained a large number of books, many, naturally, about family history. He was a writer, or, more precisely, he had had a modestly successful book first published by Faber and Faber shortly after I was born – it was reissued in 1942 as a

Penguin paperback – which he had written with William Gerhardi, a novelist, playwright and critic, born in St Petersburg to English parents, who was a renowned and pioneering supporter of Chekhov's writing in the West. (Gerhardi was also a keen supporter of the Tsarina, whom he had met as a young man, and believed that the best influence in Russia was, contrary to all normal belief, that of Rasputin who had been violently against the war with Germany, seeing – apocalyptically – the downfall of the dynasty and of the country as a result.)

Meet Yourself As You Really Are was a very early example of home psychoanalysis, one of those psychological quizzes that offers instant insights into your personality and psyche. The foreword described the book as a 'guide to self-knowledge. It takes the reader on an extensive tour of exploration into some of the less well-charted regions of his own psyche and helps him to discover new and unsuspected aspects of his personality . . . If we want to know ourselves we must not only look into ourselves, we must look outside and around us in order to get ourselves and our problems into the right perspective.'

You were asked a long list of questions about all aspects of your life, covering everything from childhood to phobias, social behaviour to daily routine. I remember one that asked, 'Do you like your bath water tepid/hot/very hot?' Others wanted to know whether you easily blushed, blanched or trembled, if you had ever had the feeling that you might suddenly go mad, or suddenly die, and whether you were sometimes amazed at the muddles other people could get into. From those answers and a scoring system, you could discover your personality type among multiple permutations (three million possibilities, the book's strapline proclaimed) leading to a number of basic key types.

William Gerhardi and my father had decided to name these different types after rivers, so you might at the end of the process discover you were the Rhine, the Nile, the Tiber or the River Thames, the latter with its conclusion, 'You're the sort of poor mutt who always pays.'

The authors did not claim any scientific accuracy – this was not a textbook of clinical psychiatry. As they pointed out, theirs was not an exact science. 'Human personality cannot be dissected, weighed, measured, preserved in surgical spirit, or dried, pinned down with needles, put under glass, stuffed or studied under the microscope. It is forever moving and changing, elusive and unpredictable.'

The book is great fun, and amused my father. I think he must have studied psychoanalysis when he had lived in Vienna and Berlin. He had certainly known Sigmund Freud there and that may have sparked his interest. He told me that as a teenager he had mentioned to his own father that he wanted to become a doctor, to which his father had simply said, 'You don't become a doctor, you *call* a doctor.' The medical profession was clearly not an acceptable choice in our family. So he saw himself as a doctor manqué, a would-be psychoanalyst.

The book was one way for him to get this out of his system, as was one of the jobs he took after he came to England in 1926 planning to make his fortune. He became a psychological adviser to the managing directors of a management consultancy, acting as a consultant to the consultants – his first job in London had been for the American literary agency Curtis Brown. He always enjoyed chatting to doctors and psychologists, and when I got married at least half of the guests he invited were from one or the other profession.

My mother, Countess Bianca Treuberg, was Bavarian, She met my father at a party in Rome in 1931, when she was eighteen and he was ten years older. Her parents had split up, as indeed had my father's parents – very unusual for the time – and she had moved with her mother to Italy, where she was looked after by a Florentine governess and eventually studied sculpture. Her schooling had been erratic, to say the least.

Many years later, I was worrying about one of the school reports my daughter had been given. I had just returned from a trip to New York, and had been staying on Long Island with that most elegant of hostesses C. Z. Guest. I told my mother I had been talking about Dora's report with C. Z., who had said, 'I don't know why you are so concerned about your daughter. *I* didn't go to school. I'm sure your mother didn't go to school. What are you worrying about?' When I relayed this to my mother she was furious. 'Of course I went to school.' 'Yes,' I said, 'but I must remind you that you have always told me that you only went for one term to the Sacré-Coeur in Rome. After which I am sure that you thought that you knew more than they did.' Wherever or however she had learnt it, she knew the whole of the *Divina Commedia* by heart. It was a source of great pride for her. She could start off at any point and carry on.

Whether or not quoting long chunks of Dante was part of her charm to my father, they married in 1932, the year after the party in Rome.

The marriage foundered rather soon, because of my father's behaviour – he was, to be frank, a serial Casanova. Like many people one knows, his entire life had been dedicated to the pursuit of pretty girls. He had married my mother because she was very attractive, and also, then, possessed some money, which was helpful, too, but neither of them knew how quickly that money would disappear.

However, they stayed together long enough to produce me. They had taken a house in Palma, Majorca, for the summer of 1933, where I was born on 24 August. Years later I went back with my wife, Josephine, to visit the land of my birth. Beforehand, we had lunch with the doctor who had brought me into the world. His own house was a huge place out in the country, very gloomy, like something out of a Lorca play.

The day was extremely hot, the dust outside was boiling. In a vast, dark room the doctor and his wife received us, tapas arrived and sangria was served. We had been asked for 1.30 for 2.00, so I thought this was the lunch. Not at all. At quarter past three another pair of huge doors opened and we went into lunch. I asked him where on the island I could find the house I had been born in. 'I knew you'd ask me this,' he said, 'but unfortunately it has been pulled down.' According to the doctor, in the early 1930s it had been a rambling country house a couple of miles outside Palma, with sixty hectares of land, and had been offered to my father for £1,000 to buy or £100 per annum rent, which is the option he chose. By the time of my return visit, the city of Palma had spread out and over the site.

Because of their separation I was my parents' only child – and remained so, since, although they both later remarried, there were no children from either second marriage.

In my father's self-analysis book, the very first question in the questionnaire was: 1) When looking back on your child-hood, up to the age of about ten, which impression predominates: that it was, on the whole, a happy childhood? If so, mark A. Or an unhappy one? If so, mark B.

I have to say that I quite enjoyed being an only child (which was the third question . . .). It meant that I became grown up at a very early age, and was treated as an adult. Blissfully unaware that my parents were separated, I never felt I had an unhappy childhood, even though I was not brought up by my father – but then in those days, of course, so many people, at least in the world I was born into, were not brought up by their parents. They were looked after by nannies and then either sent away to school or tutored at home. When my old nanny died, my mother's maid took care of me, but I still spent plenty of time in my mother's company.

Because she was a sculptor, I was raised in a world where art and literature were the most important things. She really only liked literary and artistic people. There were telephone calls at all hours of the day and night, visitors, dinner parties. It was definitely an artistic milieu, since she moved to Paris after she split up with my father and lived there with her older brother.

She was very sad that I was born on 24 August, because it meant I was, just, a Virgo, and she desperately wanted me to have been born a couple of days earlier so I could have been a Leo, like her brother, to whom she was devoted. But it didn't happen, quite luckily perhaps, as her brother was an absolutely archetypal black sheep of the family. He was Count Franz Ferdinard Fischler von Treuberg, known to everyone as Bubi.

During the war, Uncle Bubi went initially to Portugal. We heard from him periodically via Barclays Bank in London. Since he was fond of overspending, there was always considerable worry about how Uncle Bubi was managing. Somehow he did. He left Portugal and returned to Germany where, towards the end of the war, he found himself in Buchenwald – he had always been conspicuously anti-Nazi – being marched out of his cell into an interview room where sat three highly decorated generals.

When he was alone with them they told him that they were going to use what remained of their power to save him, since they had all been friends of his father, my maternal grandfather. The only way they could do this was to sentence him to death, have him released into their custody and move him out of the camp in one of their military transports to Berlin where they would deposit him with friends.

Bubi and my mother's father – although his connections had saved Bubi's life – had unfortunately been very extravagant and been obliged to sell off the family's wonderful *Schloss* and 5,000-hectare estate in Bavaria, which had been given to my great-great-great grandfather, a Prince of Hohenzollern-Sigmaringen, as a dowry for his daughter, in 1806.

My mother's father had both wildly overspent and been poorly advised. The factors who managed estates were renowned for siphoning off funds for their own benefit. Naturally they encouraged their employers in their financial ignorance. This was exacerbated by my grandfather's love of horses: he used to take them to race in different countries at great expense, but none were good enough to win a major race. My mother told me she remembered her father getting a coach and horses ready to be driven into Munich at a time when the motor car was already common. Such unnecessary expenditure was indicative of his *fin d'époque* mentality.

The lovely Schloss Holzen (which is between Augsburg and Munich) was sold in the late 1920s. It was acquired by

Franciscan nuns, and my grandfather retained the right to live in a little house nearby for the rest of his life. He used to join in their Offices every day since he loved chanting the Office and became a Dominican Tertiary.

I wanted to go and meet him after the war, once travelling to Germany started to become a little easier, but he died shortly before I was finally able to make the trip. Instead, I spent some time there with the old parish priest, who had been a great friend and companion of my grandfather. He plied me with some exceptionally good white wine. I was only seventeen or eighteen, and when I had drunk half my bottle I refused any more, thinking that I had had enough, that I was not used to drinking and that a parish priest could not afford to be too liberal with such a good wine. The priest was furious with me. 'Drink up. Your grandfather never drank less than four bottles of this wine every time he came round to see me. It's shocking that you don't drink properly. I suppose that is what England is like.'

In Paris, my mother's close friends included the Jouves. She had been introduced to Mme Jouve initially. Blanche Jouve was the first woman to gain a degree at the Sorbonne before the First War and had become a psychoanalyst. She had studied with Freud, and she was the French translator of his *Three Essays on the Theory of Sexuality* – my father would have loved to have met her. Some Paris friends of my mother's had told her about this marvellous psychoanalyst who could help her with all her problems, not that I think she had any. It was the beginning of that fashionable use of time for people with nothing else to do than to go and talk about themselves for a couple of hours every week.

The Jouves were both great intellectuals, and played a

significant part in my life. Her husband, Pierre Jean Jouve, was a poet and a novelist, a very cerebral man. He introduced me to the paintings in the Louvre and how to view them, which consisted of looking carefully at the few that he wanted to see and not looking at anything else; he said that looking at other paintings was tiring and would perhaps diminish our capacity to understand what we had come to see.

Blanche told me stories about her life. All of her male friends from the Sorbonne had been called up to fight in the Great War, and they all wrote her letters back from the front, since she was probably the only girl they knew well. One particular young man wrote a series of astonishing letters and she developed a strong attachment to him because of their content. She said that all these boys had matured very quickly because of the oncoming threat of death. None survived apart from the one to whom she was particularly attached. She was so happy that she was going to see him again after the Armistice in 1918, thinking that she would see the mature man who had written these astonishing letters. Her disappointment was great: she met neither the boy she remembered nor the man she had imagined from his writing. The trauma of his experience at the front had completely changed him out of all recognition; they now had nothing in common.

Mme Jouve was a redoubtable character, made of stern stuff, and lived well into her nineties. In her late eighties, she was living in Paris during *les événements* of May 1968. My friend Jonathan Guinness (now Lord Moyne) still remembers that when I rang her up, worried that her flat was right in the heart of the streets where the riot police and the students were fighting, she was completely unfazed and in fact rather cheered up by all the protests. 'Cela m'a beaucoup égayée,' she reassured me. 'What a game old bird she must have been,' he observed.

Through the Jouves we met the composer Darius Milhaud, who was one of the group known as Les Six (Francis Poulenc and Georges Auric were also members), and Consuelo de Saint-Exupéry, the Salvadoran wife of the aviator and writer Antoine, and the mistress of my half-uncle Werner. This social set also included Marie-Laure de Noailles, the doyenne of literary Paris, and Count Etienne de Beaumont, a great party-giver who took enormous pleasure in drawing up the list of people he was *not* going to invite. They would visit my mother in her flat in the rue Guynemer in the 6th arrondissement, alongside the Jardin du Luxembourg, where as a child my nanny would wheel me out for some fresh air.

Isabel Ryan, a South African, who was being treated by Mme Jouve for nervous problems, saw the Jouves as surrogate parents. She remembered travelling with the Jouves and my mother to Sils-Maria in the Engadine valley, near St Moritz in south-east Switzerland. There Isabel and my mother went walking in the countryside in full Tyrolean costume: white blouses, black velvet waistcoats and full skirts. She conjured up a picture of my mother on this promenade. 'The local country people they met went down on their knees and kissed Bianca's hand. The Treubergs came from Southern Bavaria, not so far away, and the peasants recognised a princess when they saw one. She was very tall and stately with ice-blue eyes and long blonde hair in plaits round her head.'

I was with the Jouves at the outbreak of the Second World War. In August 1939, when I was six, I was staying with them in Mégève, but I don't remember my mother being with us there, although she was certainly with the Jouves when they all went off to Lucerne to see the last great pre-war concert with Toscanini conducting. I heard a report that 'Bianca was great fun, but did insist on telling Toscanini how to conduct!' The story rang true; my mother saw herself as a literary, artistic, universal aunt and always had enormous reserves of self-confidence.

As war loomed, I was driven with the Jouves from Mégève down to the South of France, where my half-uncle Werner v. Alvensleben – an opponent of Hitler – had taken H. G. Wells' villa, Loupidou, near Grasse. Isabel Ryan was persuaded to drive south – 'Bianca could persuade people to do anything.'

'The Jouves had a beautiful new car,' Isabel Ryan recalled, 'a Talbot with a powerful engine and automatic gear change. Not only was I driving the car but I was also looking after Bianca's son, the young prince Rupert. The boy was in a state of shock without his mother. Kipling came to my aid. I told him *Jungle Stories*.' I remember watching the long lines of refugees walking on the roadside carrying suitcases or pushing carts laden with their belongings on, as the vast and comfortable Talbot drove past. 'Où est la guerre?' I kept asking.

While that *drôle de guerre* of the first few months after war was declared drifted by, we lived at Loupidou. Much time was spent listening to the wireless. Then in the March or April of 1940 the Jouves departed for Geneva, and my mother also left a little later to visit some friends in England, while I stayed behind in the villa in Grasse with her maid, the cook and the gardener.

It then must have dawned on her that it might be rather dangerous leaving her only child in France during what was quite clearly a difficult time. I didn't realise until many years later that there were friends of my mother's keeping an eye on me from a distance to see that I was all right. From my point of view, there I was, aged six, with the servants and no money to pay any of the household bills. We decided to head for Cannes, and so I, the gardener, the maid, the cook and the cook's little boy, marched into the Hôtel Martinez, which my mother and her circle had much frequented.

I went up to the concierge, whom I had got to know on previous occasions while my mother was chatting with friends. 'My mother's left us for London,' I announced. 'I know she's trying to get hold of us; will you find us some rooms?' Proving the golden rule that a concierge truly worthy of the name can make anything happen, he said yes, and managed to contact my mother via Barclays Bank in London to make sure all the bills were paid and that I was swiftly collected by the friends of my mother and taken to Paris.

Thereafter I travelled to London by plane, alone, which still sounds extraordinary, even now as I write it, but since I was so young it seemed quite normal to me at the time. By the time I was collected it was May 1940, and I believe I was on the very last plane of civil passengers to fly out of Paris to England before the French capital fell.

When she got to London my mother had found a flat in St James's Street, just above Boodle's Club, but before I could get too comfortable the bombs of the Blitz began to fall and I was sent off again, to stay with Madge Molyneux Seel, an old friend of my mother's, in Buckinghamshire. My mother had met Madge on a visit to England when she was sixteen, and Madge later came to stay with her in a flat in Florence.

The flat was run by Riccardo, an extremely able Florentine butler. Madge said to my mother, 'Bianca, you're being robbed blind by Riccardo. You must let me run the shopping. It's absolutely absurd.' My mother said, 'I'm sure it's not true, but if you want to I will tell Riccardo that you are now running the shopping, not that you can speak Italian.' When Madge left, Riccardo said to my mother, 'Come into the pantry.' As he opened the door, there was a pile of banknotes on the table. 'This is what I managed to get away from Miss Seel.' Madge would have overspent or been shortchanged by the local suppliers so Riccardo had intervened to make sure my mother did not lose out. And he gave all the money back to her.

Madge and my mother had remained great friends. And so I was dumped with Madge and her husband, Hans-Jürgen Roeber. Hans-Jürgen was a good-looking young Berliner who had been employed as a lutenist for my uncle Hubertus. There was a story that one day my uncle came home unexpectedly early on a wintry day of filthy Berlin rain to find – equally unexpectedly – good-looking Hans-Jürgen in bed with his wife, my aunt Helga.

Aunt Helga thought quickly. 'Oh, darling,' she smiled, 'I asked Hans-Jürgen to get into bed because it is so cold outside.' My uncle, being a man of overwhelming vanity, did not query that. He thought it was quite natural. But I think he *was* disturbed when the lutenist was enticed into marriage with this rather nice English woman called Madge.

Madge paid for Hans-Jürgen to have advanced music lessons, and he became a conductor – I remember seeing him conduct at the Wigmore Hall. He played the violin and piano, and as a small child I delighted in living in their house in the country and listening to him practise nearly all the time. I came to love music as a result of hearing him rehearsing every day. I had discovered a cupboard just next to his practice room, and I would secrete myself in there with a book, enjoying the triple pleasure of reading the book, hearing the violin, and, perhaps the greatest thrill, being hidden.

My mother visited on and off for the odd night or so, but most of the time I was looked after by Madge's old nanny, who seemed to me to be ancient, but was probably no more than sixty. Meanwhile my father was working for the Ministry of Information on short public information films, including *The Five-Inch Bather* in which the actor Richard Massingham extolled the virtues of water rationing.

Shortly after I got to the country I went to the local village school for a very short time and then was sent to a boarding school, and so my war passed far more pleasantly than it might have done given that my family name was German, which during the war was a heavy burden. I forgot my German, and I called myself simply Rupert or Rupert L. I never gave my surname. I had mixed emotions about being in England while England was at war with Germany, until my parents had explained the reasons to me. The strangeness of it all is exemplified by a display case in my library which contains my grandfather's Iron Cross and other medals and my wife's grandfather's DSO and decorations side by side.

My father had been naturalised as a British subject in 1936 – when Germany started its new federal existence in the 1950s both he and I were issued German passports, and I had to make a choice between British and Germany nationality. I chose to be British, since that was where I lived. But there was one difficult moment when I was eighteen or so and I was in danger of being called up by both the German army and the British army, and then by the Spanish army as well by virtue of having been born in Majorca.

However, during the war, in the countryside away from the

bombs falling on London, and too young to worry about call-ups, I had a really rather agreeable time. Despite my parents' separation, escaping from France in the nick of time, my German family name and a somewhat itinerant existence – all of which typified the dangers and the changes of that period – I had, oddly enough, been rather lucky. I was never disturbed by this tremendous transience. I am sure that was a help in later life, when I was part of rock'n'roll's touring circus, because I was able psychologically to cope with the incessant round of different countries, people and mores. It had been the way I was brought up.

All of my early life had a twofold effect on me. I emerged from that upbringing with the strong sense of family history and lineage and *tenue* which my father had instilled in me. As I was their only child, I was 'the lineage' that would carry on from him. At fifteen, I once asked my mother, 'What do you think the definition is of an aristocrat? I think it's pre-eminence mellowed by time.' 'Rubbish!' she said. 'It's responsibility for everyone taken for granted.'

I was also aware of the fact that we had no money. There was clearly some money to fund my parents' life, but I was not sure whether that had been borrowed from other people, or provided as bank overdrafts; by and large it was funded by selling objects, which offered a dwindling resource. Luckily credit was much easier to secure in those days. My mother had no idea about money, and my father had precious little more.

'I was not frightened by the whole concept of money,' he later wrote. 'In the formative years of my childhood and youth, I had lived in a world separated by tradition and privilege as effectively from the world "outside" – the world of professions, commerce, ambitions and struggle – as a medieval castle by its ramparts and moats. I had lived in complete security. It turned out to be a sham security, for, as I was to learn even before I reached adulthood, this world of castles, coaches, horses, liveried servants, gamekeepers, French governesses, tutors, in which I spent my childhood, was based on very weak financial foundations. The whole elaborate, yet so deceptive, edifice crumbled into dust after the First World War.

'Real or sham, justified or not, the material security of those early years gave me a carefree and detached outlook on life and the material concerns of life, with consequences, both beneficial and bad.' This, he said, had enabled him to face adversity of every kind 'with a high degree of equanimity'.

In Paris, I was told, my mother used to leave money in a dish for anyone who wanted it – a practical communist. The person who saved my mother's financial life on a regular basis was the manager of Barclays Bank in Piccadilly, just next to the Ritz. I recall many an occasion when my mother would park me in the Ritz's bar downstairs while she went off to endure a difficult half-hour with the bank's manager, but it usually seemed to be all right in the end. My mother always believed that something would turn up, and my father once said, 'If only Bianca was running the finances of some small Latin American country, she would do very well, but just running her own life seems a waste of energy.'

If my mother's sense of the value of money was virtually non-existent so, too, was that of beloved Uncle Bubi. After his rescue from Buchenwald, he became mayor of two of Berlin's post-war sectors, had moved into theatre and film production – in Düsseldorf he put on some Brecht plays – and occasionally turned up in London. He was the same as ever: I later attended his wedding to an Italian girl at the

Chelsea Register Office, and as the official stressed the importance of the vows of marriage, Bubi turned round and gave me an enormous wink.

One time, I was staying on the island of Patmos with a great friend of mine, the painter Teddy Millington-Drake. Teddy's property, two seventeenth-century houses in the village of Chora, was high up on top of the island next to the monastery of St John the Theologian. As we looked down at the activity on the harbour front below, we saw a small boy astride a large donkey, its ears poking through a battered straw hat, coming up the hill. The boy and the donkey having made their ponderous way to Teddy's house, the boy delivered a telegram, after establishing that the recipient with an odd foreign name was indeed me. I opened the telegram, written in a strange ink. It was from Bubi. The message read simply: 'Total financial support needed forever, Treuberg'. It was the archetypal black sheep's bleat.

Around the time I was leaving school, and drawing on her sculpting skills, my mother started a small workshop in Glebe Place in Chelsea, making very pretty costume jewellery cast in brass or silver. She first found an out-of-work German to do the accounts who couldn't speak a word of English, and then had to employ a friend, Benvenuto Sheard, to translate the German accounts into English. Nuto Sheard might not have been a wise choice for the role. At around the same time, Nuto, an investor in Claud Cockburn's magazine *The Week*, had been fired from his role as manager of the magazine for, according to Cockburn, 'a particularly sharp bout of what is known as "financial irresponsibility", in the course of which he removed the funds'. Nonetheless, somehow and improbably my mother's jewellery business contrived to make a bit of money.

Jewellery seemed to be central to my mother and money. She had owned one-sixth of the Brazilian crown jewels, because one of her great-grandmothers was a daughter of Emperor Dom Pedro I of Brazil. Amongst them was a splendid emerald necklace, which she kept on her dressing table. One of her friends had declared, 'I loathe emeralds', whereupon my mother picked up the necklace and hurled it out of the bedroom window into the street below. By the time they went to look for it, most of the stones had already disappeared.

I asked my mother what had happened to all the Brazilian jewellery. 'Oh, darling,' she replied. 'I left it all with Marie', who had been my mother's maid in France. 'What's her surname?' I asked. 'I don't know, she's called Marie, and *Marie, c'est une brave Bretonne*, a good honest girl from Brittany. She'll turn up at the end of the war with my jewels.' I was sceptical: 'A likely story.'

Sure enough, come the end of the war, Marie, *brave Bretonne* though she might have been, was nowhere to be found, nor were the Brazilian crown jewels. I trust that Marie and her descendants appreciated either their beauty or their value.

One day, when I was fourteen, my mother sent me to an art gallery to sell a beautiful painting by Balthus, whom she had known well in Paris. She was sitting with friends in the bar downstairs at the Ritz, and said, 'Darling, you must go to the gallery and sell this nice portrait because Mummy needs the money.'

I asked her how much she had agreed with the gallery owner – it was £40. Even at fourteen I thought £40 was not very much for such a lovely painting. Off I trudged to the bottom of Duke Street where I handed over the picture and received in return the money in the form of eight of the crisp white fivers of the day. I returned to the Ritz and by the end of lunch the money was no more. Next door in Barclays Bank, the manager, had he known how swiftly the money had been consumed, would have been furious. To me it was a good example of how not to use money. I was starting to realise that while my parents had no sense of money, I had. And I developed a lasting determination never to find myself in the same straits as they navigated on a daily basis.

2

'There is a good deal to be said for frivolity. Frivolous people, when all is said and done, do less harm in the world than some of our philanthropisers and reformers. Mistrust a man who never has an occasional flash of silliness'

Gerald, Lord Berners

My school days, like much of my childhood, had been a little unusual. When I had been staying with Madge and Hans-Jürgen in Buckinghamshire during the war, I had attended the local village school briefly. I went along for a month and then they took me away. They saw it was absolutely hopeless. I could read and write at six and a half, and none of the other pupils could. So I was dispatched to boarding school at eight.

This was a small co-educational school, Long Dene, in Stoke Poges. Thomas Gray, it is popularly believed, set his *Elegy Written in a Country Churchyard* in the parish church of St Giles in the village; the poem was displayed on a monument near the church.

I was very much an odd fish in Long Dene's pond. As an only child brought up by nannies, and to a certain extent by very bright intellectuals, I had really never met – let alone made friends with – any children of my own age (with the exception of Roger, the cook's son at the villa near Grasse). So I was somewhat mystified and even a little frightened by my coevals, and they quite probably saw me as snooty. Although I had loved all the sports at the school for my first year or so I developed asthma at the age of nine and I was unable to cope with the physical demands. There was nothing I could do about it. I did regret not being able to join in the sports, but it may have added to the impression that I was not joining in, all of which resulted in a certain tension which occasionally ended up in a fight. On those occasions I would fight back, but one part of my mind hated the actual fight, and the fact that some blows would cause pain, while the other part of me stood back and observed these two boys wasting their time over something so trivial.

My teachers, however, were very kind to me. I found it far easier to relate to adults than my fellow pupils. The music teacher there was excellent and I made firm friends with him, learning much from him and starting to learn to play the violin – strengthening a lifelong love of classical music. There was also a kindly mistress, Mary Hemingway, who taught me to read sensible books, and indeed sometimes invited me during school holidays to stay with her family on the Isle of Man, where her father was an Anglican priest. We remained in touch over the years: she later became a nun, and joined a silent order in Lourdes.

When I was about eleven it was thought important to send me to a more advanced and academically minded school. My mother had something of an obsession about co-educational schools: there were two or three very good ones in Germany, one of which was Schule Schloss Salem, established by Kurt Hahn, who founded Gordonstoun after he left Nazi Germany. Luckily, she didn't send me to Gordonstoun, since it was not co-educational, so I was saved from that experience – one I am sure would not have suited me, since I had heard from other children who had brothers there that the school operated on quasi-military principles.

Instead she selected St Christopher, in Letchworth Garden City, a progressive school, founded in the 1910s by Quakers and initially sponsored by the Theosophical Society. I think my mother was also impressed by the school's intellectual level. The Latin teacher had a great sense of humour and a fund of excellent aphorisms going back to his own schooldays in the 1890s, one of which I in turn taught religiously to my children and then my grandchildren: 'Even those of the meanest intelligence can be goaded and wearied into something approximating to thought.' My son Rudolf often found that phrase helpful in his own teaching career, although not all of his pupils appreciated it.

It was while I was at St Christopher that I heard the news of my parents' divorce courtesy of my fellow pupils' reading of the newspapers. On another occasion, one of my classmates came up to me with a copy of the *Daily Express* – we were meant to read only *The Times* – which contained a report of a plane crashing on take-off at one of the London airfields. There was a photograph of my mother emerging from the plane, which was in flames behind her, holding a bottle of champagne. The journalist had commented that it was an odd choice of item to rescue. 'But what else would you do with a bottle of champagne?' she had said, with commendable, and typical, sang-froid.

I was happy at St Christopher, and extremely pleased with myself, since by and large I often came top in lessons. But after three or four years there I decided I wanted to leave for a more conventional schooling. Such children as I had met in the holidays went mainly to Eton or Downside.

I approached my mother and asked her if, in the summer of 1949, when I had passed my Higher School Certificate (the qualification that would be replaced by A-levels a couple of years later), I could go to Cambridge and be tutored for a scholarship to Oxford. This idea had been instigated by my history teacher at St Christopher sending me to Cambridge once a week to be tutored in history by a marvellous, very old-fashioned Edwardian spinster, Miss Anderson-Scott, a teacher who was associated with Girton College, the time not yet having come when women could be members of the university.

My two years in Cambridge were the greatest possible fun. I was found digs by Frances Cornford, the Bloomsbury poet, who was a friend of my mother's. She knew a charming old German philosopher, Dr Strich, whose wife was looking to rent a room or two in their house. She looked after the house and cooked the most delicious Prussian fare, a great difference from St Christopher, which was not only co-educational, but also vegetarian (as indeed I am told it still is even now). The professor and his *Frau* had two very old-fashioned daughters, Lore and Sabine, who were a little older than me and seemed to have stepped straight out of a novel by the nineteenth-century writer Theodor Fontane. My mother was happy that I was lodging with a family like the Strichs, in a sensible, protective environment.

At Cambridge I made many friends including two or three whom I still see today, and I got to know Monsignor Gilbey, the chaplain to the university's Catholic undergraduates, and one of the most well-known and admired priests in Britain.

With additional tutoring in Latin from a Fellow of King's College I prepared myself for the Oxford entrance examination, a perverse choice, it might seem, since I was enjoying myself so much in Cambridge, but by chance I knew more people – either friends of my parents, or friends of mine – who had been at Oxford than Cambridge, and of course it amused me that I was going to have two years at Cambridge before three at Oxford.

I had decided to study medieval history. Classics appealed, but I had only started Greek in my last year at school, and so would, I thought, have made it difficult to catch up. Had I been to Eton or any similar school, I would certainly have read Mods and Greats at Oxford. But that was not possible, although I took Latin as my second subject for my Higher Certificate and continued studying it.

I wanted to go either to Magdalen or Christ Church. When I took the entrance examination, Magdalen gave me a Demyship. I was very happy with the choice, and in the autumn of 1951 I was installed in excellent rooms in the New Building.

Magdalen was famously strong in history. A. J. P. Taylor was a Fellow, as was the medievalist K. B. McFarlane. He was one of the people who marked my Finals, and was angry that I didn't get a first. He later published a book of letters in which I appeared in a passage describing a visit he had made to the tombs at Wertheim: 'I have a boy, R zu Loewenstein-Wertheim-Freudenberg, from this family, who is a complete rascal.' What he meant was that I was not paying enough attention to his words of wisdom. *Tant pis.*

I did not get on with my main tutor. I did not like him – he was very nervous and chippy – and he didn't much like me either, but that was perhaps the only thing with which I was unhappy at Magdalen. It was unfortunate, but certainly not the end of the world.

My parents had taken it for granted that I would get into Oxford. In fact they would have been horrified if I had failed to do so. My mother would come down with a friend perhaps a couple of times a term; my father visited once or twice over the three years I was there. Before the war, his half-brother – my half-uncle – Werner v. Alvensleben had been at Hertford College; among the friends he made at Oxford had been Adam Trott zu Solz, a diplomat who was part of Count Claus v. Stauffenberg's 20 July 1944 plot to assassinate Hitler. My half-uncle also became great friends with the Chaucer specialist Nevill Coghill. And so I was invited to join Professor Coghill at high table off and on.

I was at the time reading a lot about Byzantine history and at one dinner found myself sitting next to an extremely ancient don, Professor Dawkins, a professor of Modern Greek. I asked him, 'When were you last in Turkey?' and he said, 'Oh well, um, I was last there before the Young Turks rose.' The Young Turk Revolution had taken place in 1908, so that gave me to think, sitting there in 1951, a difference of only forty-three years, how close we are to the past, and how short the time was to that completely different world, now vanished forever.

When my relations and their friends talked about 'our war', they meant the Great War of 1914–18. When I went up to Oxford there were many older students who had fought in the war which had ended only six years earlier – a war within touching distance – young men who had been away to fight and only now could come back to do their degree.

My own skirmish with military service – the moment when I was in danger of being enlisted by three different national armies – had ended in an honourable truce, as I was saved by the asthma I had first developed at Long Dene. Just before I was called up by the British Army a young man had died after an asthma attack during training. Although his doctors had recommended that he shouldn't be called up, the army had originally overridden the medical advice. Now they were being very careful. Although my asthma was not all that bad, in their cautiousness they thought it was not a risk worth taking.

The aftershock of the war rumbled on. Rationing for most foodstuffs, tea, bread, sweets and sugar, remained in force, clothing coupons had only just been abolished, and for at least my first year or so at Oxford, restaurants were still limited as to what they could charge: five shillings was the highest for food. Restaurants with expensive decorations and good service were allowed to charge an additional cover charge, the maximum of which was 6/6, so at the Ritz or Claridge's you would have paid 11/6 for lunch or dinner.

Nevertheless I contrived to have a jolly existence. I was not a diligent student, very much to the contrary. I did not work very hard because I enjoyed the life in Oxford and making friends, talking and chatting, and all the other things which Cardinal Newman, in his book *The Idea of a University*, thought were equally important for young men going to university, to be around intelligent people, even though it might not be strictly part of the course that they were following.

I basically worked for one day a week, the day I had my tutorial. That one day I diligently walked to the Sheldonian, parked myself there, and read through part of what I had to read and wrote part of what I had to write – or sometimes even less (my tutor later recalled I had 'read out' one essay from an entirely blank sheet of paper). I always rather slyly managed to arrange my tutorial for the late afternoon on Thursdays so that for the rest of the week I floated about, went out and got drunk with friends, and enjoyed myself tremendously. I made many lifelong friends: Desmond and Jonathan Guinness, Michael Dormer, John Pollington (now the Earl of Mexborough) and Dickon Lumley (later the 12th Earl of Scarborough, now deceased).

There were a few girls at Somerville, LMH, St Hugh's and St Hilda's, or studying at the Ruskin School of Fine Art. Other girls could find themselves at a strange kind of finishing school, or a typing school called Cuffey's. One of the Cuffey's girls I knew was Serena Dunn, now Lady Rothschild (sister of the writer Nell Dunn).

There would be no mixed colleges at Oxford for another twenty years. Despite my mother's ardent support for co-education, I think I rather liked the fact that Magdalen was all-male, partly because historically it had always been like that and I was aware of the fact that before 1870 all the Fellows had to be celibate and the rest of them had to be in orders of the Church of England. To me that aspect of Magdalen formed an integral part of the history of Oxford.

I spent quite a lot of my time going up to London – if we missed the train back, taking a taxi for the fifty-mile journey was a very expensive five pounds. Coming back from London one night after the college gates were locked I had to climb back in with the assistance of a suitable, though booby-trapped, lamppost: I have a mark on my arm where I cut it on one of the vicious spikes the college had placed around it to prevent precisely that means of access after hours.

I had a great deal of fun with my friends. With Desmond Guinness I visited Faringdon House in 1951, the year after the death of Lord Berners, about whom I had heard so much from Desmond, whose mother, Diana Mitford, had been a great friend of his. Lord Berners, Gerald Tyrwhitt-Wilson, was an idiosyncratic avant-garde composer (he was called 'the English Satie' and Stravinsky much appreciated his work), painter, novelist and all-round surrealist. Regular dinner guests at Faringdon included the Sitwells, Aldous Huxley and Cecil Beaton.

Lord Berners had left the very nice house to his younger boyfriend and heir, the equally unconventional Robert Heber Percy, known as 'the Mad Boy'. I had met Robert once or twice casually without getting to know him to any great degree, but he was a closer friend of Desmond's, whose family he knew very well. He invited Desmond and me for a weekend. Faringdon was in the Vale of the White Horse, twenty miles or so south-west of Oxford, and we decided to go there by horse. It was not a completely insane idea. I much enjoyed riding; Desmond was a very good horseman, who had also ridden while in the army.

It was rather longer a ride than we had anticipated. It seemed to take a day or two, although in reality I can't imagine it took more than four or five hours. But it was great fun. The main difficulty of this rather strange, though most enjoyable, trek was how to complete it because of having to navigate our way through villages, gates, fields and private property. But we managed it and arrived late at night.

Staying at Faringdon was well worth the effort. We had a

hilarious weekend, Robert Heber Percy being extremely amusing and, between games of charades, regaling us with stories about Lord Berners, the 'Last Eccentric' as one biography of him was titled: he had placed an advertisement in the personal column of *The Times*, declaring that 'Lord Berners has left Lesbos for the Isle of Man', his telegraphic address was 'Neighbourtease', and he dyed his pigeons various colours, most notably pink.

He kept a clavichord in the back of his Rolls-Royce, once had a giraffe as a pet and in the grounds of Faringdon had built Folly Tower, which he was delighted to describe as 'entirely useless'. The epitaph on his gravestone read, 'Here lies Lord Berners/One of the learners/His great love of learning/May earn him a burning/But praise to the Lord/He seldom was bored'. We certainly had not been. We decided to have our horses picked up for the return journey and came back to Oxford more pragmatically but less interestingly by train.

On another occasion I had heard from Prince Henry of Hesse that he was coming over to England and wanted to see Oxford. So Desmond Guinness and I took him on a tour and thought a good trip would be to go to Cornbury, an Inigo Jones-style seventeenth-century house near Charlbury. At that stage Cornbury belonged to Togo Watney of the brewing family, who in a rather convoluted way was married to Desmond's stepmother's sister.

The house was most impressive, and the paintings were staggering. They had not yet had to be sold off. Prince Henry was a talented artist himself; his pictures were almost the size of miniatures. He was impressed by the fact that the art collection at the house included a small Botticelli of which he had never heard. It had originally been owned by the

Pucci family of Florence, and was the first painting to feature forks (which the Puccis had introduced to Europe). A year or two after we had visited, it was sold back to Emilio Pucci, of the silk pyjama fame.

A rather more unfortunate happening surrounded the bizarre attendance of Constantine Nicoloudis, who, as his name suggests, was Greek and whose father had been a diplomat and accompanied the royal family to Egypt and South Africa during the war. The father was married to an extremely tough and energetic wife née Manos, a niece of Aspasia Manos, the commoner who married King Alexander I of the Hellenes in a secret ceremony following an elopement (King Alexander died in 1920 after being bitten by two monkeys. The ensuing fateful war against Turkey conducted by King Alexander's father Constantine I, who returned to the throne, led Winston Churchill to write that 'it was a monkey bite which caused the death of those 250,000 people').

Constantine arrived at Oxford in a blaze of notoriety, not quite publicity, since that did not exist in the form that it does today, but we all knew that he was coming and that he had some link with the Greek court. His early days as a student were symbolised by what we took to be his trademark: a batch of elegant white five pound notes which we thought he had come by from his parents or perhaps was even his own money. Constantine was a regular gambler. When he lost he became very mournful and dejected, and then his mood would lighten and the five pound notes became apparent once more.

It emerged that he had forged some cheques belonging to Teddy Millington-Drake. Teddy's bank in London had spotted the forgery after noticing a rather suspicious person coming in to cash them. Desmond and I could not believe that this was true because, although we occasionally went up to London with Constantine on the same train, we thought it would have been impossible for him to go to the City to cash a cheque in the time available, since banks in those days were only open between ten and three. So we thought that it was simply a somewhat hysterical response of Teddy's.

When the police politely came on a number of occasions to question us about Constantine, we stood on our hind legs and protested violently that he was an abandoned Greek in a sea of enemies. This went on for a week or two before Desmond said, 'Well, I'm afraid it's true, because he has forged some of my cheques as well.' We had to change our tune, apologise to Teddy for having imagined that he had invented the whole thing and generally to understand that this delightful and entertaining companion of ours had acted criminally.

The story ended in the expected manner. Constantine was sentenced to jail but after three or four weeks was released.

The next time I saw him was many years later, by which time he had married a rich English girl, and was spending his time taking choice guests sightseeing in Athens. We were wandering around the Acropolis, and I noticed Constantine with a gaggle of tourists. One of the people we saw him with cheered me by saying, 'Constantine, Constantine, you *must* show us the Seven Horsemen of the Acropolypse'!

I certainly learnt a lesson from that experience: that you have to look much harder than one expects to be necessary before you are able to trust people where money is involved.

During one of the summer vacations I went on a trip to Europe with Michael Dormer. In Biarritz we met an amazing couple. The male half of the couple was the most elegant man I'd ever seen: tall, white-haired, with a moustache and an eyeglass. He was a Baron Wrangell, a nephew of the General Wrangell who commanded the White Armies after the onset of the Civil War in Russia in 1918. Baron Wrangell was picked by David Ogilvy, the founder of Ogilvy & Mather, to feature in one of his early ads as 'the man in the Hathaway shirt' sporting an eyepatch, which made him instantly recognisable.

George Wrangell's father had been the Imperial Russian ambassador to Rome during the First World War. When the Revolution started his father's brother, the General, told him, 'Don't come back, stay where you are. We will get all our money out, because what's happening now is a nightmare. This Revolution is far worse than anybody realised.' But George's father responded, 'No, I am an ambassador and I work for His Imperial Majesty. There is no question of deserting Russia in its time of need.' He went back to look after his property, but didn't get a penny as everything that belonged to the family had been looted.

When I met George Wrangell he was married to one of those terrifying rich American ladies; this particular specimen of the breed was called Kathy. The Wrangells were often in Europe and by and large lunched on dry martinis and the odd olive. George himself, I discovered later, had been an admirer of my mother's in Rome in the late 1920s. He and Kathy had bought a house in the south of Spain where they spent part of the time and the rest of the year they stayed at Claridge's, the Ritz in Paris or in their apartment in New York. George rather took to me because of knowing my mother and we also made friends with Kathy.

She once said to Michael and myself that she had been married previously to a whisky manufacturer – 'panther piss', she called it – who had made a lot of money. 'So then, boys, I had three other husbands, two of whom I shall never mention to anybody they were so dreadful, and the first one was a darling but he died of drink.'

I spent my twenty-first birthday in Biarritz with Michael, and the Wrangells gave us dinner. Afterwards we went off to the casino, where she said, 'Here you are, kid. Here's a chip for your birthday.' When I looked at the chip it was a £1 counter, which I promptly put on number twenty-one, and equally promptly lost.

Kathy was hilarious. She took us to a party thrown by American friends of hers, Tiny and Chuck, at their very grand house. The party, which we rather enjoyed, was equally grand. But Kathy got fed up, went up to Chuck and Tiny and said, 'This is a ghastly party. I'm taking my guests away before they throw up in corners. The drink was disgusting, the food was worse, and your guests were ugly. Goodnight.' Michael and I did what I call the 'double wink', winking simultaneously at her and the wretched hosts. Next day, two o'clock came round, and whom did we see coming for a luncheon party but Chuck and Tiny. 'Oh darlings,' Kathy welcomed them. 'What a great party you gave for us last night. We had such fun. We couldn't stay too late because George was getting tired...' It was a swift education in social diplomacy. And about a world that no longer exists.

The education I was meant to be undertaking was a three-year course. In my last term I did become somewhat more interested in studying and asked the historian Karl Leyser, who was the person in charge of me, whether I could stay on for an extra postgraduate year. He said no. I mentioned this to another historian, Raymond Carr, whom I knew and who was at New College and he said, 'Well, you can come to New

College', which was very generous of him, and which I have never forgotten. I was very grateful to him, but although my parents would have been very pleased if I had become an academic – although I think my mother might have expected me to become an unsuccessful literary critic – I very much wanted to earn money, to avoid the fragile financial uncertainty of my parents, and by that time I had already had a job interview.

I went to the Oxford University Appointments Board to look for a job one May afternoon before my Finals. There I was seen by a Mr Escrit, who asked me, 'What do you want to do?' 'I don't know,' I replied, 'but I want to make money. Where can I make money?'

Mr Escrit rummaged through a selection of leaflets and picked out two or three for me to look at. One was for the Metal Box Company in the Midlands: the job paid £600–£700 pounds a year. They were based in Perry Wood, not far from Birmingham. It sounded a long way away from the life I was used to.

The second job offered some similar salary, but was up in Leeds, ever further flung as far as I was concerned. And the third was for a company called Bache & Co., New York stockbrokers, but they only paid £400 a year. 'Where's their office?' I asked. 'Well, it would be in London.' That did it! My mind was made up. And the fickleness of fate had determined my future.

In my first year with Bache my salary was indeed £400 with two weeks' holiday and work every other Saturday morning. I learnt how to deliver securities and transfer deeds in the Square Mile. And I also learnt how to work in an office with a simple calculating machine, which in those days was nothing more than a glorified abacus. One day I was asked to work out

the amounts payable to each of our registered names, computing the gross amount of dividends payable and the various
deductions and withholding taxes. I got them all wrong.

The manager took me out for a cup of coffee at the Lyons
Corner House below our office. In a certain amount of pain,
he asked me whether I had learnt any form of book-keeping
at college. I regretfully answered, 'No', but told him that,
having studied medieval history, I could give him detailed
information on the regnal dates of the Byzantine emperors
between 867 and 1204. Therefore I suggested it might be safer
for my arithmetical work to be checked by someone else in
the office.

Within three years of starting work in London with Bache,
I found myself getting married. I was living at Boodle's in
those days and had been invited to a dinner party. The host
had been a good friend of mine when I was studying at
Cambridge but was a little dull. I thought to myself, 'Well, I'll
go there if nothing better turns up.'

Nothing better did turn up and so I attended this dinner for
six or eight of us. My date, as it were, was a very glamorous
blonde who had arrived driving a beautiful grey Bentley
convertible. We got on very well, and after the dinner she gave
me a lift back to Boodle's in the Bentley.

The following week I was giving a cocktail party for my
cousin Johannes Thurn und Taxis and thought to myself that
this glamorous blonde, Josephine, would be a perfect person
to invite. She came – and we got engaged two months later.
Needless to say, it transpired she had also decided to go to the
original dinner only if nothing better was on offer.

It turned out that our paths had crossed before that dinner
party. Josephine thought that she had seen me once across the

room at a fancy dress party in Chelsea, and that she had been invited along to a party I threw with Desmond Guinness in my rooms at Oxford, but we had only been briefly introduced and so had not had a chance to make any significant impression on each other.

She had also noticed my father, and his second wife, Diana, when she lived near him in Earls Court. Not knowing who he was, she and her mother had often speculated on the identity of the tall, distinguished, well-dressed gentleman and his pretty wife they saw in the restaurants on the King's Road.

Josephine was two years older than I was, and had gone to the ballet school at Sadler's Wells (run by the formidable Ninette de Valois), the precursor of the Royal Ballet School. But she was too tall to continue studying ballet past her teens and so to her great sorrow had to give that up. Instead she went to Rome where she studied singing for three years and had a wonderful time in the Rome of the early 1950s. But she had grown bored with Rome and had returned to London, where she had been working for the Social Services department in the East End while she thought about what she was going to do next. Although at the age of twenty-six she was, by the mores of those days, deemed very old to be unmarried, she had not felt under any especial pressure to find a husband.

After getting engaged, we went through a difficult phase, as I was earning relatively little money. Josephine's parents were initially very set against the idea of us getting married. It was understandable. Her father had fought in the war and been badly wounded; her grandfather had been a general commanding a battalion of Grenadier Guards in the First World War. The family were less than pleased about their only daughter wanting to marry a young German who was apparently penniless but also a Catholic: Josephine's family, the Lowry-Corrys, were staunch Ulster Protestants.

When we were married, at the Brompton Oratory in July 1957, it was a mixed wedding and we could have organ music but no singing and no nuptial mass, only a blessing. What was quite entertaining about our wedding was that – as, unusually then, we were both only children and both our sets of parents were divorced – although all four parents were there they stood at least two yards apart from each other in the receiving line, which was hilarious. They were there, they were affable, but they certainly were not going to speak to each other.

3

'Experience is what you get while looking for
something else'

Federico Fellini

Despite my first, unsuccessful, stab at computing dividends during my early days with Bache & Co. in London, I had discovered that I was in fact fairly numerate. I could, for instance, read and create balance sheets and so did possess the necessary semi-technical skills, and I had a good memory. Most importantly, if I became a deal-maker I realised what could be ceded. Essentially I had an instinctive sense of money, one which I had certainly not acquired from either of my parents, and I had found a métier where I could gainfully employ those instincts.

When I started work, the enormous shifts in the British class system were still ten or more years away, and I had no real inkling that there would be any significant change, even after the Suez Crisis of 1956, which in retrospect marked the first cracks in the foundations of the existing Establishment. When I left Oxford all the good jobs in the City were by and large still being taken by public schoolboys, as were those at the Bar and in most professions and avocations.

In the 1950s nobody I knew who went into the City or insurance or law had a starting salary of more than £300 or £400 a year, on which in a strange way one was able to live – if you had a roof over your head and a friendly bank manager.

At the time we married, Josephine had a little money, with £6,000 of which she had bought 4 St Leonard's Terrace – the street ran parallel to the King's Road in Chelsea, just opposite Wren's Royal Hospital. It was a charming house in a charming street, very tall and thin, somewhat like a vertical flat, with five rooms one on top of the other. Later, when I had made some money, we moved and bought a house in Holland Villas Road, which had, as I remember it, ten bedrooms and a large garden, for £35,000.

I was still extremely committed to reaching a position where I could avoid the financial insecurity that my parents had always lived with. Josephine remembers my 'dogged determination'; she, too, came from a family which had lost the bulk of its estates and money. At one point they had owned a large portion of the ground rents of Belfast and large estates in Shropshire. By the time I met her it had nearly all been lost in a couple of generations, through the selling of land and ground rents at the wrong time, and although Josephine, who would otherwise have been a significant heiress, accepted the situation fatalistically, she was saddened by seeing the family let it slip through their fingers. As in so many similar cases, they knew how to run an estate but had little commercial experience in terms of maximising its value.

The increase in my earnings had initially come about when I became a commissioned rather than salaried man for Bache.

Since the only European office Bache had apart from London at that stage was one in Paris – where the director was Hans Czernin, whom I and my parents knew – the company thought that they could capitalise on my connections by sending me to help open a number of other continental offices for them and attracting new clients.

This required a substantial amount of entertaining, which was never an issue for me. I was then very gregarious and I enjoyed any lighted candle. I think we were known as a 'merry' couple. Even when we had little money we would find a way to have people round for dinner every few days with a larger dinner party every fortnight or so.

Josephine was not and is not gregarious in the way that I was, so all the entertaining was a strain for her, especially at the beginning. She found it particularly nerve-racking because of the pressure on all the women to wear immaculate *haute couture* outfits. Josephine improvised by finding a Cypriot dressmaker round the corner who helped run up her clothes from good materials.

Of course the entertaining did take up quite a lot of time, but being a stockbroker did not require me to be hard at work on a consistent basis. The hours were tiresome because of the time differences between stock exchange opening periods but apart from that my colleagues and I were often sitting at our desks twiddling our thumbs, or in my case gossiping with my friends.

I had started my worldly life in my late teens. Both at Cambridge and at Oxford I had met and made friends with people who were by and large a minimum of two or three years older than myself because they had been through National Service, from which I had been exempted because of my asthma. I attended their parties and went to stay for weekends.

Compared to others of my age, I was well travelled. At the age of fourteen I had travelled to New York on my own. My mother had remarried. Her new husband, Peter Rosoff, was an American publisher, and I was duly dispatched to join them in their Manhattan flat for my summer holidays, crossing the Atlantic on the liner RMS *Queen Elizabeth* (and back on the *Queen Mary*). I travelled out in cabin class and in my cabin got to know a history professor at Pennsylvania University who specialised in American warfare. With a shared interest in history we got on very well, and I got on equally well with his very attractive daughter who was also on board.

My mother was much in France and Italy where on visits I met her always intriguing circle of friends. Consequently, by the time I was married I already had a busy social life in Rome, Paris, London and Munich, and my employers rather shrewdly realised that I might be a good person to seek business from these people – the head of their 'foreign' department was a socially mobile Roman who was very keen on landing gilded and generous fish.

The next few years were something of a *dolce vita* period as, courtesy of Bache, I enjoyed a very jolly international time, spending three months of each year in Rome, the heartland of that very *vita*, and Milan, and a further two to three months over the winter in St Moritz. I was also in Germany for shorter periods, perhaps one month twice a year overseeing the opening of the Bache office in Frankfurt. Here the emphasis was on administrative details added to chatting to potential clients. In Germany wealthy people were looked after by local banks, while in Italy much of their wealth was abroad.

Wherever I was in Europe, I felt quite at home, and thanks to my parents' facility with languages, which they passed on to me, was quite happy chattering away in French, Italian and German. My mother was completely fluent in all three, as well as English, my father also, although his Italian was never as good as my mother's. When he spoke, he had the mildest of German overtones. You might equally have thought he was Swedish, and my mother Italian. Theirs was the accent of European cosmopolites.

Even though there was work to be done, the predominant mood was cheerful and the greatest possible fun. How could it not be? Here I was at the turn of the decade from the 1950s to the 1960s, newly married, staying in glamorous hotels with my glamorous wife, and getting to know swathes of the people who were then known as café society. My cousin Johannes Thurn und Taxis never quite got that appellation right. He called it 'coffee society', which in a way was the same but different.

Whenever I was in St Moritz, not being much of a skier I spent much of each morning chattering on the telephone to other equally less sporting people. Marella Agnelli, from a princely Neapolitan family, wife of the Fiat chairman Gianni, rang me very early one morning saying that she had to go to Rome in her private plane to look after her niece, who was dying of cancer and was alone, and therefore would I tell our friend in common Marie-Hélène Rothschild that as a consequence she would not be able to go to the dinner party that Marie-Hélène was giving that evening.

A good two or three hours later I rang Marie-Hélène for a little gossip, which centred around a discussion of her various aches and pains, ending with her enunciating – as if it was a profound truth – the platitude about good health being the most important gift one has. I saw my opening, and told her that Marella had been obliged to go to Rome to look after her poor niece, who not only was in the latter stages of a terminal cancer but had both recently been widowed when her husband had been killed in a car crash and was bereft of her father who had also died of cancer the week before.

There was a short pause. 'Et mon dîner?'

I was also now the father of two small sons: Rudolf, who was born in 1957, very soon after we got married, and his brother Konrad, who followed a year later. When we were in London I was unable to be as close to the children as I would have liked since I was working for American stockbrokers. My hours were very difficult to blend with an active father's role. Bache had to base themselves on New York time, since the market did not close there until eight o'clock in the evening London time, and one of the wretched employees had to take down the prices and talk to the people who gave one orders late at night, all of which was extremely irritating from the point of view of my social life.

I managed to work it out reasonably well, but even so it meant I was rarely home before seven or seven thirty, and I suppose I only saw the children for any reasonable time at weekends and said goodnight to them most of the other nights. That was, of course, far from unusual for the time.

Once, when we were staying at Bembridge on the Isle of Wight, my father visited for tea. The boys were absolutely angelic. As my father left, he said, 'So nice to see you, children.' Rudolf and Konrad said their goodbyes with immaculate politeness – any other mode of behaviour would have been inconceivable to them at that time – but Rudolf remembers he could not really bear the pretence and so burst out with, 'Oh, Grandpa, we don't really like you, we're only pretending.' My father hooted with laughter.

He had also remarried: his second wife was Diana Gollancz, the daughter of the publisher, Victor. She died young, in her forties, from cancer of the brain, and in tribute to her he wrote *A Time to Live, A Time to Die*, a very personal and moving second book. 'It is difficult,' he wrote, 'ever to catch the fragrance of a human person. There are in our life a few climacteric moments when we must make a choice. We do not always recognize these moments for what they are, and only when looking back do we realize the full significance of a choice made at a particular time.'

The boys would come along on the European trips for their holidays, though in those days they stayed with their nanny in pensions close by where Josephine and I would be put up in a grand hotel. There was no question of the boys staying with their parents in their hotel – not because we asked and were refused; we wouldn't have dreamt of asking.

The lifestyle we enjoyed established itself into a pleasant seasonal pattern. Whenever I was working for Bache at the office that they opened in Milan – and of all extraordinary times they wanted me there in August, when anyone with any money deserted Milan and headed for the seaside – we were able ourselves to escape for weekends in Venice, staying at the house of my colleague Bino Cicogna, who was made manager of the Milan office, or, indeed, with other friends and fellow guests who included the novelists Maurice Druon and Nancy Mitford, Victor Cunard (Nancy's cousin and *The Times*' correspondent in Venice) and Harold Acton, a writer, poet and a witty conversationalist as original in his own way as Lord Berners had been. He was frequently thought to have been the model for the character of Anthony Blanche in *Brideshead Revisited*, but although he was friends with Evelyn Waugh at Oxford, Waugh always denied that he had been the inspiration.

One night at dinner we were discussing mutual acquaintances, and the conversation moved on to the subject of which hotel in Venice everyone preferred. One of the guests mentioned, 'Well, my sister-in-law *hates* the Metropole.' Harold wagged his finger sternly. 'Oh, Arthur, I never associated you with sisters-in-law' . . .

Lunch would be consumed on the Lido in the various cabanas near the Excelsior Hotel, served by footmen from the various houses in white coats and golden heraldic buttons. One scorching day I remember we were presented with an entirely cold repast. Bino's sister Marina turned to her mother with a blazing eye and pained expression. 'No, Mamma, la colazione deve *sempre* essere calda e cremosa.' Marina insisted on her breakfasts and lunches being both warm and creamy until she embraced the delights of dieting with zealous fervour.

The Contessa Anna Maria Cicogna had a palazzo on the Grand Canal and was a great defender of the city, leading a 'committee to save Venice' as early as the 1960s ('Venice is dying slowly, like an old lady, without tears or laments,' she said at the time), but we also visited her in Libya. Her father had been the Italian governor of Libya and had constructed a wonderful house there. We set out on expeditions to the Roman remains at Sabratha and Leptis Magna, where, on the edge of the sea, a table had, as on the Lido, been set for a sumptuous lunch.

Spending so much time in Italy, especially in Rome, I was

able to continue developing my love for and knowledge and understanding of classical music. My tastes, as at Oxford, leaned towards Bach, Mozart, Beethoven, Schubert and Brahms. I had less interest in twentieth-century composers, although I had records of *L'Après-midi d'un Faune* and *Le sacre du printemps*, enjoyed Hindemith, and was familiar with the music of Les Six, partly because of the Jouves, who knew that group of composers so well. They had also introduced me to another great friend of theirs, the cellist Maurice Gendron, who used to come over for dinner, bringing his cello with him, and often played some unaccompanied Bach cello suites. I always found it fascinating to watch him perform because he smoked while playing, with a *mégot* permanently planted in his mouth. I was riveted waiting to see what would happen as his cigarette burnt ever lower since his hands were otherwise occupied. Somehow he always managed to snatch it away just before it burnt his lips.

Nineteenth-century Italian music and operas I only really came to know after getting married, because Josephine had studied singing and knew all of the nineteenth-century repertoire extremely well, Verdi, Rossini, Donizetti, Puccini. We often went together to Covent Garden and then to see opera in Rome, where we first heard Maria Callas in *Norma*, at the Terme di Caracalla.

I met Maria Callas later in Paris both before and after her involvement with Aristotle Onassis, and found myself sitting next to her at lunch and dinner a few times. She had become an unhappy woman. Even as a young man I could see this great genius was truly miserable. It was terribly sad. A vast talent, shaken by an unfortunate love affair. Nothing more complicated than that. Any other young man or woman who had had an unhappy love affair would eventually have moved on, but for somebody with such a highly developed and tense emotional side, it had a much more serious effect. We spoke in French, her voice low and melodic, and she in person, striking and attractive, though not classically beautiful.

On another later occasion Josephine and I were invited to a small dinner by M. et Mme Bory. He was a property developer who owned Fauchon, the grand grocer's and foie gras specialists in the Place de la Madeleine, and was very socially active. The guests included Maria Callas, Ingrid Bergman and the Duchess of Windsor ... You would have thought this would have been one of the most fascinating dinners in the world. But not a word was spoken by any of these three great ladies – they were each so powerful that they were struck dumb in each other's company.

Bache's plan of sending me to Europe worked. As I made new acquaintances through my existing network of friends or met other guests in the hotels, I was able to bring new clients to the firm, including Stavros Niarchos, owner of the largest shipping fleet in the world: I tried to get part of his account and ended up managing some of his English securities through the London office.

I also became great friends with Arturo Lopez-Willshaw, a Chilean whose fortunes – ironically for a man who was such an aesthete – derived from the sale of guano, the phosphorus- and ammonia-rich droppings of seabirds that was highly prized, and valuable, as a natural fertiliser up to the end of the nineteenth century.

I first met Arturo at a cocktail party given by Lady Abingdon when her husband was attached to the British Embassy; my cousin Johannes Thurn und Taxis had taken me along.

Arturo modelled himself on a miniature edition of Louis XIV and was a committed collector of walking sticks with Fabergé handles and, more importantly, great Louis XIV furniture. I remember he once saw me walking very fast through the hall at the Palace Hotel at St Moritz and stopped me to say, 'Now then, Rupert, one important lesson I must teach you: never walk fast, because it will look as if you have something to do!'

Among his many elegant possessions, Arturo had acquired a motor yacht called *Gaviota IV*, originally built in 1931 for the head of Reynolds Tobacco. Josephine and I joined the Lopez-Willshaws onboard many times. It was the most luxurious boat that one can imagine. A maximum of eight guests were looked after by a crew of twenty-six, all English, bar one French sailor, who was expected to speak all other languages. Josephine was particularly impressed by the fact that our friend Perla Mattison (wife of the banker Graham) brought along two vast cabin trunks, and that she and the other ladies on board changed for dinner into a different *haute couture* dress every single night of the voyage.

Arturo was married to a charming Chilean, Patricia, but it was widely known that theirs was an amicable marriage of convenience. When I met him, Arturo had just broken up with a young boyfriend, Tony Pawson (whom Josephine knew). Tony was an English man about town whom Arturo had put up in a grand flat in Paris. The story was that Tony's mother had said to a friend of hers, 'It is so marvellous about my son Tony. We thought he only had about £200 a year, which is all we give him. But he must have found a marvellous job in Paris; look at all those suits he had made.' Not only was Arturo funding Tony's sartorial elegance, he had bought him a pink Rolls-Royce complete with a black chauffeur. Arturo later told me that he chose a pink Rolls-Royce because it was instantly recognisable and so he would always know what Tony was up to.

However, Tony had been superseded by a new companion, Baron Alexis de Redé. At that cocktail party Arturo, Alexis *and* Tony were all in attendance. Alexis and Arturo were key lumps of sugar in the coffee pot, or *cafetière*, of that society. Arturo had met Alexis during the war in New York, where Alexis was attached to one of the large stockbrokers. It became apparent to Arturo that Alexis was very bright and had a sound head for business and so not only did he become a loyal companion, he also looked after the Lopez fortune.

The person best placed to describe Alexis was Alexis himself. After his death in 2004 I helped publish his memoirs. 'I dislike fervour and enthusiasm,' he said. 'I do not like noise. Very often, I remain silent, for silence has its own dignity. I listen for the nuances that stir behind the Babylon of general conversation. I relish comfort, style and luxury. I dislike men who do not wear white shirts in the evening. Many such things I dislike.'

Alexis became a good client of mine, and it was he who first invited me to a dinner with Maria Callas. Alexis suggested, one winter in St Moritz, that I should look around for a small merchant bank to buy in London. He encouraged me by telling me both that the purchase would be interesting to him and that he thought merchant banking would be a better long-term career for me. At the time he gave me that advice he was right, and the advice sensible: stockbrokers, even in the United States, were partnerships, and there was not the opportunity to make huge amounts of money off flotations. Being a broker I didn't see myself continuing just being a broker trying to get new accounts for the firm.

However, had I in fact stayed with Bache I would probably have ended up benefiting enormously from the subsequent change in the financial climate by the public offering of Stock Exchange partnerships. But I have no regrets about accepting Alexis's advice. When I returned to London I set about looking for a merchant bank to purchase.

Within a year or so I had found a suitable answer in Leopold Joseph & Sons Ltd. It was a small merchant bank – I always considered it to be the smallest grade I bank whereas others may have felt that it was a good fish but in grade II. The brothers who owned it did not possess the ambition to channel themselves into being one of the great players although in New York their counterparty was Salomon Brothers and so they were well known internationally.

At the time the most important stockbrokers were Merrill Lynch and Bache and half a dozen other American brokers, while in England Cazenove, Panmure Gordon, and Hoare were in the same sort of business as the existing merchant banks: Rothschild, Baring's, Hambros, Philip Hill, Warburg's, Schroders.

The smaller merchant banks like Leopold Joseph were smaller simply because they did not have big clients, who were attracted to the larger banks able to raise significant sums of money. In those days the City was going through a very difficult period. Taxes, it must be remembered, were at 83 per cent above £2,000 and above £2,000 a year any unearned money – dividends or interest – carried an additional surtax of 15 per cent. Which it is easy to see adds up to 98 per cent of somebody's income. The consequence of this was that unless it was really necessary the average merchant bank director hardly worked at all on Mondays and Fridays. He would come in, dressed in tweeds, at ten, have a long, highly liquid lunch and leave at four.

Leopold Joseph, the founder of the bank, had been born in 1863 in Michelstadt, a town in the Odenwald region southeast of Frankfurt. Leopold had moved to Frankfurt aged about ten. His father, a trader who had started providing banking services to his suppliers, had decided to formalise the arrangement and set up his own bank, A. S. Joseph, in the city.

Leopold Joseph joined the family bank, and rose to associate partner by his late twenties, at which point the bank was being run by one of his cousins. A. S. Joseph got into difficulties and collapsed, and Leopold relocated to London where he worked for Reuters as a reporter on banking matters, acted as City correspondent for the *Frankfurter Zeitung* and spent the 1910s as joint manager of the London office of Swiss Bankverein.

By 1919 he felt ready to set up his own institution, Leopold Joseph, which evolved through various partnerships, and then was expanded to include three of his sons, Bertie, Oscar and Teddy. Despite some losses during the Depression, the bank survived and flourished, so that the family members enjoyed a life of some comfort. Leopold died in 1940 – the *Financial Times* noted that 'the City loses one who by his personal charm, strength of character and business acumen had become greatly liked and respected among the banking community'.

Of the three brothers, when I got to know them, Oscar seemed to me the cleverest and the one whom any organisation would have been pleased to have as a director. Bertie, the eldest son, was somewhat lacking in matinee-idol good looks and not particularly interested in meeting new friends and clients, while Teddy was more of a social animal.

Oscar Joseph apparently did not believe in spending time or money on entertaining during business hours. The story goes that one day the office manager was astonished to hear that Oscar had asked for 'two coffees and a glass of port'. On further investigation this turned out to be a Chinese whisper: he merely wanted 'two copies of our latest report'.

The dilemma faced by the bank after his death was that none of Leopold's sons had children, and, with no family succession, the three brothers spent much time throughout the 1950s and 1960s pondering the future of the firm. Various mergers were explored and approaches considered, but nothing had been resolved by the time the bank came into my sights.

In the official history of the bank, the story is told that Alexis and I sat leafing through a copy of the *Bankers' Almanac* looking for likely candidates, and deciding against any banks with knights of the realm on the board of directors as we thought they would be unlikely to sell. At Leopold Joseph we had a personal contact: a second or third cousin of Josephine's, Freddie Lowry-Corry, was working there. That it had been founded by a German called Leopold (my father's Christian name) was a neat coincidence.

Alexis and I initially made a bid for an 80 per cent holding in the bank, which was rebuffed as the Josephs did not want control of Leopold Joseph heading overseas. Undeterred, we then gathered a group of friends and clients together to form a consortium to purchase the bank. They included Anthony Berry from the Kemsley newspaper family – which at one time owned the *Sunday Times*, alongside the *Daily Sketch* and the *Sunday Graphic* – and Jonathan Guinness, whom I had known since Oxford (and who is still one of my closest friends). As well as being on the board of the family brewing company he had worked in the City at Erlanger's and moved to the board of Philip Hill when they took Erlanger's over. While on the board of an investment trust he had talent-spotted two bright young men at Rothschilds, Louis Heymann and Richard Cox-Johnson. Both Jonathan and I felt that we had to have some hard-working professionals involved, and he heartily recommended them both, since he was certain that they would want to leave Rothschilds where they felt they were being underpaid; he was right.

The news that we had acquired the bank was, pleasingly, announced on 23 July 1963, the 100th anniversary of Leopold Joseph's birth, and followed by a dinner at the Café Royal to mark his centenary.

We agreed that the Joseph brothers (who were then in their sixties, while most of the consortium were thirty years younger) should stay on the board for three years to teach us the ropes, but I soon found that some of those ropes were rather frayed. To be honest, they taught us very little. They were really like a nineteenth-century version of a merchant bank and, though a good one, out of touch with current practices.

I was sent over to New York to report on the banking contacts we had there. I returned somewhat horrified by the fact that the Josephs had not secured their lending arrangements with Salomon Brothers, who were their principal money brokers there, in the way that was normal for banks at the time. The profit that banks in London usually looked for in the transactions of taking and lending vast sums of monies was a quarter of 1 per cent. With Salomon Brothers Leopold Joseph took one-sixteenth of a per cent.

When I relayed this, the Josephs were not at all put out. They said, 'We're perfectly happy with our arrangement with Salomon Brothers. Old Mr Salomon and our father were great friends; one went to New York and one went to London and we trust them completely.' This, alas, was not good enough for us, and so we had to tighten up a few of those relationships and to try to open up a few more. At a board meeting in September 1966 the three brothers stepped down together, finally ending the family involvement.

At Leopold Joseph the work was much tougher than it had been with Bache, which was a vast organisation. I had to work harder, but I was making much more money. All to the good. There was a trade-off, of course. I no longer enjoyed those long months in Europe. I did have one or two 'deals' with European counterparties and some real estate transactions in Paris which allowed me to travel a certain amount, but the *dolce vita* days were over.

Nevertheless, I found new acquaintances in the banking world who were equally entertaining. I was a keen bridge player and joined the Portland Club, reputed to be the oldest bridge club in the world.

The form was that members could take in a guest on a Monday night and the guest would be placed on the right of our club chairman. One evening, in the early days of running Leopold Joseph, I took as my guest 'Jack', an extremely competent, and very nice – though somewhat gung-ho – American investment banker, who was the son of the senior partner of a large, respectable New York investment bank. Accordingly he sat next to the then chairman, Quintin Hoare, of the bank of the same name.

Halfway through dinner, Quinnie opened a bleary and

Angostura-tinged eye, realising that he was obliged to talk to this savage visiting from over the water. 'I suppose you work in Wall Street?' he asked. 'Yes sir,' answered Jack brightly. 'I certainly do. I am at my desk at seven every morning, have a quick bite for lunch, sit and work doing mergers and acquisitions until six or seven every evening, and return home at eight. I usually go to the Regency Club to play a rubber or two of bridge and my wife Cathy, she'll probably go riding.'

Quinnie studied him, 'Goodness me!' he said in a deeply bored voice. 'I get to my desk at about ten most mornings and go upstairs to our dining room at around midday, have a few drinks and a damn good lunch with a few friends, then get back to my desk for a little while to sign my letters, but I am never at this Club later than about 3.30.

'I'm the head of a family bank which started in 1672, and we have been very keen on keeping the bank for the family, so that however stupid they are, at least they can get a job. Studying genetics, as I have always had to do out of necessity, I have realised that most of my relations are far too stupid to run a bank and the few that *are* able, I teach carefully that the one thing they have to do as bankers is to lend money to people that don't really need it at a higher rate of interest than what we have to pay for the deposit. That way we have survived.' My American friend, I am sure, reported this *in extenso* to his father.

I met the developer Walter Flack – whose head was being sculpted by my mother – and raised money for his company in the City. There was one hilarious meeting at Warburg's with Siegmund Warburg. Before it started we overheard him asking his secretary with whom the meeting was scheduled: was it Alexander Fleck, the industrialist, my man Flack, or Friedrich

Flick, whose family owned Mercedes? At one point we over-heard Warburg snap at a hapless minion, 'Are you talking about Fleck, Flack or Flick?' Finally, having apprised that the client was in fact Flack, Warburg leant across the table and said, 'Mr Flack, if everything went well for you, what would you have really liked to do with your life. My dream is *not* banking. If I could I would have a garden to cultivate, like Voltaire, outside Geneva, walking, discussing literature and philosophy.' Walter Flack answered, 'I'd like to have a horse in the Derby declared the winner after two objections were raised.'

I also had to learn to deal with the Bank of England. There we were controlled by Mr Hilton Clarke, principal of the Bank's Discount office. Any misbehaviour in the banking system was monitored and stopped by the Bank of England if Hilton Clarke raised his eyebrow. I recall an occasion when the directors of Leopold Joseph, including the three brothers, were all summoned by him. Jonathan Guinness arrived a little late and after a while it became apparent that a tin of condensed milk in the pocket of his mac had found its way upside down and therefore was leaking through the hole he had punctured in it. What Mr Hilton Clarke made of that he did not share with us.

So at work I was in a world rooted in tradition. Even in the 1960s I would wear a bowler hat and had I been in the money market I would have worn a tall hat. Some elements of City life were evolving, however. We realised that business would have to follow the American line, much more serious, much less time to oneself, no swilling down of dry martinis in the middle of the day. Even during my first visits to New York for Bache in the 1950s I had noticed that people by and large didn't drink at lunch whereas in London that was the whole point.

Outside the Square Mile there were significant changes afoot in the life of English society, which altered the way that people dressed, thought and ran businesses, and it was imperative that it did, otherwise it would have become moribund. Social life was changing. The presentation of debutantes at court ceased in 1958. Many large houses were being sold. Normal dinner parties for fourteen to twenty guests in dinner jackets gave way to a much more casual approach.

Josephine and I had dinner with a great friend of ours and when we arrived at 8.45, apart from our hostess all we noticed were about ten people sprawled on sofas or sitting on the floor not speaking a word. Josephine and I looked at each other and said, 'Now we understand what it means by people being stoned', and from then on we got used to the fact that at certain parties – not all, by any means – this would be repeated, and more and more people we knew started behaving in the way that became so popular in the 1960s.

Five years on from the purchase of Leopold Joseph I was contacted in my office by Christopher Gibbs. We had met, in that wonderful French phrase, *dans le monde*, a party here, a party there, in no particular way. Christopher was a bright young man about town, from a large and rich family, whose wealth, like Arturo Lopez's, had originally been built on guano.

Christopher knew Mick Jagger, and Mick had asked him to find somebody to advise the Rolling Stones on their financial situation, which was not good. Mick had realised that he had made a tremendous mistake in listening to the approaches of Allen Klein. The Stones' first manager, Andrew Oldham, had no professional qualifications at all, but was a breezy young man who arranged their first gigs and thought that he might make some money out of the Stones for them and himself. By comparison, Allen Klein was a very knowledgeable, highly intelligent, if unconventional chartered accountant, who'd set up on his own in New York and specialised in giving advice to rock musicians.

But it was now clear to Mick that something was wrong. He was deeply worried. He knew the group was doing well and had a good contract with Decca. Their singles and albums were selling strongly, and they were playing to enthusiastic crowds. He couldn't understand why they weren't seeing a penny. By and large they had no money. They were all overdrawn.

Unhappy with what was happening, Mick turned to Christopher for help. From Mick's point of view Christopher was an Establishment figure, a young man from the upper class, which in those days still mattered tremendously in the City; he had the requisite entrée into the City. Christopher may have had the entrée, but he could find no one interested in looking at the finances of what virtually everyone in the City viewed as degenerate, long-haired, and, worst of all, unprofitable layabouts. When Christopher spoke to me he said he had talked to a friend who worked at a large firm of accountants, 'and I outlined what we were talking about and he said they weren't able to do it'.

Any large firm of accountants of the day, whomever he had gone to, be it Deloittes, be it Price Waterhouse, would have had the same attitude. Christopher had also introduced the Stones to a firm of solicitors, who were hopeless, which he realised after a certain time. So he telephoned me.

'Could you look after the financial side of these friends of mine, Mick Jagger and the Rolling Stones?' I just said, politely, 'Let me call you back tomorrow morning', not having heard of the Rolling Stones in any connection with anything that I might do or want to do, let alone thinking that this could form the basis of a business association.

As I had no real idea who the Rolling Stones were, I made some telephone calls and Josephine told me the background of their success, and reminded me of the famous *Times* editorial which had been written the year before by William Rees-Mogg following Mick and Keith's conviction for drugs possession, the leader article headlined 'Who Breaks A Butterfly On A Wheel?'. I did remember the piece. I, of course, had been on the side of the wheel.

One of the calls I made was to a friend of ours, Peter Denman, who was related to the Erlanger banking family. As managing director of the bank he had been central to the marriage between Erlanger's and Philip Hill Higginson & Co.

It turned out that I had met Mick a short time before at Peter's house in Chelsea. Cara, his wife, used to throw the new style of informal parties, to which we went. It was one of the occasions when we walked into the room and found everybody stoned. And one of the people whom I had tripped over was Mick.

4

'Only sick music makes money today'

Friedrich Nietzsche

The second time I met Mick Jagger, in the autumn of 1968, was via a far more conventional arrangement, planned and by invitation, at the house that he had bought on the Chelsea Embankment, where he was living with Marianne Faithfull.

I had placed a number of calls to business contacts to try and gain some sense of what I might find myself getting involved in. Chrissie Gibbs had given me some useful advice. He told me that the image Mick projected was what he needed to satisfy the Stones' fanbase, but that he was far more intelligent than the image and that his ideas were well worth listening to. Yet I still did not know quite what to expect when I headed to Cheyne Walk.

I sat waiting in Mick's drawing room, reading a newspaper. Despite the upwardly mobile address, the décor of the house was extremely sparse, the rooms quite bare. He had not yet bought much furniture, but had picked up a few Moroccan objects from his trips there, probably much cheaper than they would have cost on the King's Road.

Soundlessly, Mick slipped into the room, wearing a green tweed suit. We sat and talked for an hour or so. It was a good long chat. His manner was careful. The essence of what he told me was 'I have no money. None of us have any money.' Given the success of the Stones, he could not understand why none of the money they were expecting was even trickling down to the band members. That was the key point, and explained the paucity of furniture in the house. He had nothing to buy any pieces with.

I wanted to make it quite clear that I had not expected much wealth, but that I did expect that what he wanted someone like me to do for him was to establish a structure whereby he could indeed make some money. Even at that point, I said, without yet having looked at the documents and papers, I thought that the exchange control of the time meant that he would have to leave the country.

I also established my own credentials, letting Mick know that I knew Bill Paley, then the chief shareholder of CBS, socially, and that I had good banking arrangements with most of the leading banks in Switzerland.

At the end of our conversation it was clear to me that although our discussion had been quite professional, Mick and I had also clicked on a personal level. We got on very well straight away. There is something that exists between people which is an understanding or non-understanding of what a person is really like. I certainly felt that Mick was a sensible, honest person. And I was equally certain that he had been taken for a ride, and that I represented a chance for him to find a way out of a difficult situation.

I left saying that I would discuss things with my partners at Leopold Joseph, but I also invited him to come over to our house one evening a few days later. I had discussed with Josephine my thoughts on that initial interview with Mick, and so asked her to receive him when he arrived, as I was intrigued and amused to know whether she agreed that Mick was somebody with whom I ought to be doing business. She remembers that her first impression of Mick was that he was smartly dressed, with a large hat over his long hair, trousers that looked as if they had been made out of a patchwork of tapestry, mixing stripes with a floral pattern, and white patent leather shoes.

While I remained upstairs, Josephine invited Mick into the drawing room and asked him what he would like to drink. He didn't seem to want anything, but she persevered, and offered him some sherry, which in the end he accepted. So they sat down with their glasses of sherry and chatted. As I had done, Josephine found Mick very easy to talk to. After a quarter of an hour or so, she said she would go and find me. She came upstairs, like a canary returning from the coalface, and reported that she thought Mick was charming. Having secured – to her relief and mine – Josephine's approbation, which was important to me, I came downstairs to continue the conversation.

As Mick and I talked more, I realised that, looked at sensibly and without being distracted by the showy trappings of the music business, the problems that Mick and his fellow Stones were experiencing were not unusual. They were straightforward, in fact. I was intrigued.

On the surface Mick and I might have been seen as unlikely business associates. Certainly so far as the Stones' music was concerned I was not in tune with them, far from it. Rock and pop music was not something in which I was interested or listened to. Josephine was hardly any more interested in pop music than I was, but she had a greater awareness of what was going on from reading the popular newspapers, and she had been to one of the Beatles' concerts in Paris where she experienced the awe and terror of being in the middle of the hysteria that surrounded them.

I had first come across the Beatles (and naturally, not being particularly aware of them, when I first heard the name of the group in my mind the word was spelt like the insects) when we stayed with some cousins in Kitzbühel and as a gift Josephine brought along the latest Beatles LP for our hostess, Sunny Auersperg – later to become, after remarrying, Sunny von Bülow – who was delighted to have it. Sunny played the record while we were there and so I had heard some of the Beatles' music. Their music was sufficiently harmonic to be acceptable to people like me who only liked classical music. I only really took against rock'n'roll when I heard the Stones.

One of the first times I heard the group play live was very shortly after meeting Mick at one of the theatres in London's West End which had started putting on rock concerts. Mick had invited me to see them perform, and Josephine and I sat at the front of the dress circle.

What impressed me enormously was the quality of Mick's performance. I thought it was first class, even if the music itself did little for me. I could immediately understand why the band were such a draw for the public.

I remember being amused by one aspect of the show that night. At a point when Mick was completely energised and excited, he told the audience, 'What are you all sitting down for? Get up and let us know what you think.' How odd, I thought. Surely he must be impressed by us sitting here in silence to admire and take in everything that was going on, rather than getting on our feet and not being able to see properly.

The offer to look at the Stones' financial situation had come at a very good time for me both professionally and psychologically. I was becoming, to be perfectly frank, rather bored with my work at Leopold Joseph, and had come to the conclusion that running a small merchant bank was not going to satisfy me if it was my sole activity.

The alternative, it seemed to me, would have been to go and work for a company like Bache in America, where there was good money to be made in the banking and investment advisory work. Although the prospect of making money was certainly attractive, it would have entailed uprooting my family, my children, my home, everything that was part of my life, a life I rather enjoyed. I was not at all convinced that I wanted to do that. The conversation with Mick seemed to offer a glimpse of a new direction and a problem that I could use my particular skills to unpick.

Many rock musicians prided themselves on their anti-Establishment credentials, but by the time I was sitting down to chat with Mick in Cheyne Walk there had been something of a coming together between the fringes of the rock world and the British upper class. The younger members of the aristocracy, who previously might have been dispatched into the military, the City, a diplomatic career or the priesthood, had discovered a new career by dropping out – a human response, perhaps, to the alarming decline and dispersal of the agreeable country houses they had been born into and the 98 per cent taxation which had impoverished their parents – so that hanging out with musicians, whom they actively courted and introduced into their world, was a rival use of their time and energy.

I remember Harold Macmillan once saying that when he was young he met 'everybody' since there were parties in private houses night after night where young MPs like himself got to know 'the world' and how sad it was that that was no longer the case. It is odd to think that nowadays the new rich are so much richer than the old rich ever were, even making allowance for inflation, but that the old aristocratic life which was so emulated by the new rich of 100 years ago is no longer, save for very rare exceptions.

The Stones were very much part of the shift in society and Mick in particular had enjoyed crossing the portal into a different social world. With Marianne and Christopher Gibbs, he had been to stay with Desmond Guinness at Leixlip Castle in Ireland, for example. As a result of such adventures, the musicians became less scornful of the Establishment and the potential money-making machine through getting to know these younger, empathetic scions of aristocratic families. The elder members, mind you, as a general rule still disapproved.

Through these social interactions the musicians became much more open to accepting the fact that not all upper-class people were necessarily stupid and unpleasant, and the upper-class people slowly got round to thinking that musicians were not all depraved and foolish.

I am sure that, even if the Stones' music did not thrill me, I was more open to and less judgemental about their world than others in my position as an active director of a merchant bank. Working with musicians was not such a quantum leap for me. I had grown up in an artistic milieu. My mother was a sculptor, and I had been brought up in a world where art and literature were highly regarded. I had spent time in and enjoyed the company of my mother's friends, who blended together in a similar way, though in a different generation, the Establishment and the aristocracy with powerful artistic and bohemian temperaments.

In my role with Bache I had learnt how to operate and do business with people from a range of backgrounds and cultures. And I was still only in my early thirties. For those times I was, if not a unique specimen, certainly a *rara avis* amongst the traditional and soon to be endangered species that inhabited the square mile of the City.

My work with the Stones formed part of what would become a new way for bands to do business. Previously band managers had either been concert promoters, roadies with ambition or friends who were at a loose end and found themselves with granny's inheritance to fritter away.

I flatter myself by thinking that when I started working for the Rolling Stones I opened a completely different door for other people to find a career in music management, because the musicians themselves were beginning to realise that the same newly well-off friend who had stumped up a hundred pounds to buy a van or purchase a better guitar was now cheerfully taking half their profits, even more cheerfully when success arrived. It was a period when many bands were starting up, and most of those lost money or, rather, did not receive the money that should have been coming to them.

The brighter musicians knew that things had to change. They now realised that they were running a business, and they had to start thinking in a businesslike way, which they themselves I think despised: the idea of making money in a conventional way and abiding by all the tax rules and regulations and the exchange controls then in force.

I was fortunately able to move on from the constraints of those preconceptions and see the potential benefits for both parties – unlike my partners in Leopold Joseph, a number of whom were initially horrified until we had discussed the matter very fully. It was the two working directors who had previously been at Rothschilds who were the most appalled, whereas Jonathan Guinness, Tony Berry and Alexis de Redé were not at all surprised.

These other partners were much concerned that the Rolling Stones were inappropriate clients for Leopold Joseph and that they would bring very little reward but a high level of anxiety to a conventional and small merchant bank.

They saw nothing but the disadvantages of getting involved with people whose character and the image they projected were diametrically opposite to those of the City of London. This was an age when to the Establishment rock bands were categorised as 'long-haired layabouts', and the music industry as a fringe activity with dubious accounting practices. A small merchant bank like Leopold Joseph was anxious not to get caught up in anything which in any way seemed to be on the boundaries of finagling.

However, I eventually managed to persuade them that the financial problems of a prominent rock band were no different in essence from the problems of any other financial organisation which sought advice in the City of London. Indeed, I also made the point that many directors of any number of well-known companies listed on the Stock Exchange led unconventional lives.

The situation was proved in a very depressing way by Mick's

friend Jann Wenner, who wanted to start up the magazine to be called *Rolling Stone*, and had invited Mick and, in so far as the other Rolling Stones counted, the other band members to buy 49 per cent of the shares. Mick could not raise the money required, which was £5,000. He asked me if Leopold Joseph would lend the money to him.

My partners were not prepared to give an overdraft to Mick because there was no security (in their minds) to back it with, and the magazine was an unquoted start-up. That highlighted for me how dire the situation was. I did finally get my partners to agree that we would have given Mick an overdraft, but their agreement did not come in time. The opportunity was missed, and the Rolling Stones did not end up with half of *Rolling Stone*, which was a great shame. Obviously Jann Wenner would have changed the percentages later on, but the band would have made a healthy profit.

For a long time there would continue to be stout resistance to my work with the Rolling Stones within the financial institutions. I remember even as late as 1973, a few years after the demise of the Beatles as a touring and performing group, when the Stones became, unchallenged, the most famous band in the world, the Swiss bankers Hensch telling me, 'We couldn't possibly have people like that in our banking halls.' My response was to say, 'You're wrong. We're in the middle of a recession. These people are on the up and up. The world is changing.'

Mick and I quickly built up a good relationship. After the first two or three business meetings, I realised that there was something exceptional in his make-up, that his personality was able to convert what, to me, was a rather uninteresting trade, that of an itinerant performer, into something far more intriguing. And although our senses of humour were quite different we were able to notice and enjoy each other's.

Alongside my work examining and studying the mountain of documents involved in the Stones' financial affairs, the friendship between Mick and I evolved, and I got to know Marianne Faithfull, who had a sort of wayward lost-girl persona. Eventually I even became less concerned, although never totally, about the more criticisable aspects of his behaviour: the chucking of invitations, the late arrival at dinners and parties, even though I found it very difficult. I prefer to be both punctual and punctilious, although my mother was the complete opposite: I would arrange to meet her for lunch and she wouldn't turn up until it was too late since I had to be back in the office by 3 p.m. in time for the New York Stock Exchange opening.

A year or so after Mick and I met, Josephine and I had been invited to spend Christmas at Warwick Castle by Lord and Lady Brooke, great friends of ours. We suggested that they might ask Mick and Marianne to stay for two or three nights and they agreed to invite them, too.

Arranging this was something of a risk on my part. I wanted to see how Mick behaved. I knew that he was intrigued and at the same time impressed by the aristocracy and that he would certainly have his views about their strong and weak points. And I think he in turn realised that I would have a different view about morality and what was fit and proper.

Though the stay was entertaining for many reasons, there were difficult moments. The plan of introducing Mick and Marianne into the house party did not work out very well since Marianne stayed in bed 90 per cent of the time; Mick tried to do his best in the tricky situation that this created. The couple had in any case got off on the wrong foot by arriving extremely late in an old white Bentley flying the Green Flag of the Prophet, with Alan Dunn as Mick's assistant and driver (he still looks after Mick to this day). Sarah, Lady Brooke, had left in a huff having poured water into Marianne's bed, which she had also turned into an apple pie. The reason she gave for this was that she thought Mick and Marianne would serve as a bad influence on her children . . .

Mick had already made a number of friends with people who owned large houses where he had been to stay, but there the hosts were interested in the music and were moved by the rock'n'roll. Whereas the likes of Lord Brooke didn't care much for rock'n'roll but enjoyed the glamour. And nor did I, or many of my friends.

Baron Alexis de Redé, my partner in the consortium that had acquired Leopold Joseph, was a great and elegant host. On one later occasion he organised a splendid dinner with his companion, Arturo Lopez-Willshaw, at Versailles. Could he invite Mick and his new wife, Bianca? I asked. Alexis was not keen. This was an era when Bianca thought it was very dashing to wear a full ball gown for lunch and turn up in jeans for a ball. In England nobody thought twice about such things. In France, however, they minded tremendously about *les apparences*.

In the end Alexis decided to invite them. Bianca asked me, 'Will we be well seated?' 'You will be *appropriately* seated,' I told her, 'but by the way, if dinner is at ten it will be at ten, and they won't wait for you.'

Mick had his own particular interpretation of these social party rules. Around the same time – still earning a well-deserved reputation for chucking parties or arriving very late – he and Bianca invited Josephine and me to dinner at their house on a Sunday evening. We were staying with friends in Hampshire, by whom we were encouraged to stay until after dinner because of the afternoon traffic. I telephoned Mick to say we couldn't make dinner that night. He and Bianca were *outraged*. 'We've bought the fish, it's all arranged.' I don't think he saw the irony.

Mick was never awkward in social situations. He was charming in fact, and was a sought-after guest. Among many of my friends at home and abroad who formed part of café society, a good side of it was a curiosity about people with a level of celebrity (indeed, fashionable designers and hairdressers were beginning to be frequently invited to events). They were fascinated to meet Mick and see him close up; they could put their hand into the cage.

I realised that one of the things Mick liked about me was that I could open gilded doors. And so I did quite a lot of that. Early in 1969 Mick and Marianne decided they wanted to go on holiday in Brazil with Keith and Anita Pallenberg, somewhere that was both hot and exotic. I organised a trip for them through my friendship with Walter Moreira Salles, a powerful Brazilian financier and politician, who arranged for them to stay in a large plantation house which he owned 300 miles or so north of Rio. I later learnt that the countrified feel of the ranch led directly to Mick and Keith writing the basics of 'Honky Tonk Women' while they were staying out there.

Given our burgeoning friendship, it was perfectly logical that Mick and Marianne would be invited to the White Ball that Josephine and I held in July 1969.

The social pages of the newspapers seemed to think there was a certain amount of anticipation about the ball. A couple of weeks before, the *Daily News* ran a short piece which announced, 'All of social London talks of nothing but Prince and Princess Rupert Loewenstein's ball on July 3' – sheer hyperbole, of course, but I did like the last sentence: 'However, if you're not invited it's not the end of the world. Just almost.'

There was a charming review of the ball by *Vogue*. 'In bright Kensington moonlight, about four hundred and fifty guests laughing and dancing joined the revels. Dancing continued until dawn in the green and white conservatory designed by David Mlinaric; every room was decorated with white vinyl cushions; nearly all the guests wore white.'

That 'nearly all' was a reference to Marianne turning up in black. A correspondent from *Women's Wear Daily* (still going strong, although rebranded for the digital age as *WWD*) wrote that 'Marianne Faithfull went almost unrecognised with the blonde hair wrapped in a silver turban and wearing a long black beaded dress. "Some people just have to be different," a little blonde in silver and blue mini over pants commented.'

'Guests walked through the house,' the same reporter continued, 'into a Victorian garden under a grass green marquee. Past the tiny white tables and chairs, and the white painted gingerbread gazebo hung with ferns and huge white Japanese lanterns was the dance floor.'

Various guests caught her eye: Jacqueline de Ribes 'in her fringed Nina Ricci', the Maharajah of Jaipur, Victoria Ormsby-Gore 'looking like Alice in Wonderland' and Peter Sellers in his long black wig.

Peter Sellers was the first show-business person I had got to know well, although he was not a client. We had been intro-duced through Grace, Countess of Dudley, who had become a close friend – she was an elegant and highly educated Yugoslav who had previously been married to Prince Stas

Radziwill. I used to play bridge with her and on one weekend visit to the house which she and the Earl of Dudley had near Amersham, among the guests were Peter Sellers and his first wife, Anne.

We found we shared a sense of humour – though like many comedians he was *moderato* rather than *allegro* off-screen. He had a house in Italy near Sabaudia on the coast between Rome and Naples. One time Josephine and I were staying in the incredible palazzo created nearby by the Countess Volpi, the widow of the founder of the Venice Film Festival. Peter joined us there one evening. Someone remarked that there was a full moon, so the Countess looked through the window but could not see it. She summoned her butler and demanded, 'Fioravanti, dov'è la luna?' Peter and I both thought this was wonderful and from then on he would often sign off letters to me, 'Dov'è la luna?'

In one letter he apologised for not being able to meet up on one particular Sunday, because he would be 'up north seeing an old friend of mine, Teevy Splurnes. He has the rare distinction of being an ex-hangman's mate. Nowadays he runs a Corset Emporium and our housekeeper is an exclusive patron. I understand she is at present down to her last pair of Splurnes. So I know you will understand why we have to collect them for her . . .' This was Peter back to his Goonish inventiveness – he did suggest that I might help Spike Milligan, and I enjoyed two or three hilarious lunches with Spike, but also it became clear that there was no money to look after . . . On the other hand Peter's own business manager, Bill Willis, was extremely helpful in explaining to me some of the inner workings of the business of show business, and, indeed, was one of the people I turned to for advice when Mick first contacted me.

Josephine and I went to Peter's wedding to Britt Ekland in February 1964 – which was less than a month after they had met while both staying at the Dorchester Hotel; by the time of the White Ball they were already divorced. What we found extraordinary was that we were the only people at the wedding who were friends. The rest of the entourage were the hairdresser, the hairdresser's boyfriend, the dressmaker, the boss of the hire car firm and various film directors and producers. It was a glimpse for me of the hermetically sealed world in which a superstar – which Peter had just become – can become trapped.

In an album of cuttings about the White Ball, I came across a newspaper diary piece from earlier in 1969 which I had completely forgotten about. 'Almost everyone would grab the chance of appearing in a film these days,' the unknown diarist declared. 'But I have discovered one reluctant actor. Prince Rupert von Loewenstein [*sic*] was offered a part in *The Magic Christian* by his friend Peter Sellers, who stars in this film. But he has decided against this chance of becoming a cinematic idol. His last reported stage appearance was as a spiv in a revue for charity while at Oxford.' In any case, Equity rules would doubtless have jeopardised my chances of appearing in the film.

Back at the White Ball, the Skatalites and Yes, who were providing the musical entertainment, had brought their own sound systems and there were, inevitably, some complaints to the local police station. Of the press cuttings about the ball, the headlines of virtually every one used the word 'rave-up', an expression that, if you did not know in which year the party had taken place, could carbon-date it almost precisely – 'A right royal rave-up' was the *Daily Mail*'s contribution.

Looking through the cuttings it seems that the calls to the police – a hundred calls according to the *Sun* – emanated almost exclusively from one particular neighbour. 'The Prince's garden was like a fairground,' she told reporters the following day. On the other hand, one of the ten nuns of the Society of the Holy Child Jesus immediately next door informed the press, 'We were told about the party so we knew what to expect. We've no complaint.'

The *Daily Mail* had been unable to quote me directly in their piece ('Prince Rupert was not available for comment. He was asleep'), but later a *Daily Express* reporter had managed to find me stirring 'in a royal-blue silk dressing-gown in the peace of his Holland Park home'.

My response was to explain 'I know it can be a terrible bore if there's a frightful racket next door and you're trying to go to sleep. But one doesn't give a party to annoy the neighbours. It really wasn't as bad as all that . . . The stillness of the night made it sound worse.' I then excused myself, saying, 'I really must have a bath and shave before going out to dinner. It'll be a quiet affair, I believe.'

The very next day I was in Hyde Park for what was defi-nitely *not* a quiet affair: the Stones' outdoor concert, where Mick, clad in the same milkmaid outfit he had worn to the White Ball, read extracts from Shelley's *Adonaïs* in memory of Brian Jones, whose body had been found early in the morning of the day of the White Ball. Not quiet, but not yet deafening. In these early days the noise levels at the concerts I had been to were not overbearing, nor impossi-ble to bear.

The noise phenomenon only hit me when the band started playing in the larger venues where they overcompensated for the size of the venue; that is they overcompensated for the people in the good seats.

I had entered what, to me, was an alien world. However, I never felt uncomfortable. On the contrary, I felt excited at seeing such a magnificent phenomenon. There was no doubt about it, the Stones in performance were most impressive. I certainly thought so at Hyde Park and when I had first seen them live in the West End. Above all I had noticed how professional they were.

It was that afternoon in Hyde Park that Mick and I discussed how easy it would be for him to manipulate the huge crowds. I was reminded of this potentially destructive power when I heard about the tragic event at Altamont later that same year, when a young man, Meredith Hunter, was killed, even though that incident had been provoked by the involvement of the Hell's Angels as security guards.

For the first time I was made aware of the extraordinary power of the band's music and in particular of Mick's charisma. I was struck by the way that he was able to project himself on to a mass without any enormous skill in the disciplines usually required for a singing career. He had none of the technical expertise of the brilliant singing stars I admired – Tito Gobbi or Boris Christoff, say. I realised that what Mick had was 'star quality'. That was the phrase I had been searching for.

5

'I know how men in exile feed on dreams'

Aeschylus

As I started examining the intricacies of the music business I felt something of the pioneer spirit. For a while there was nobody else taking on a similar role to the one I was undertaking for the Stones. Shortly afterwards, of course, other groups of professionals emerged, who could also see the way the entertainment world was changing.

These were the lawyers. Lee Eastman and his son John, who represented Paul McCartney after the Beatles' break-up, were both entertainment lawyers (Paul met his wife Linda Eastman as a direct result). Jim Beach, the long-time manager of Queen, also started out as a lawyer. It was a predictable path: the small groups who turned into the big bands were obliged to find good lawyers, who then scented profits and transformed themselves into managers, in precisely the way Allen Klein, a qualified accountant, had spotted the chance, realised it was enormous and exploited the opportunity with not just the Rolling Stones, but also the Beatles.

It was Mick who had introduced Klein to John Lennon a few weeks before I met Mick. After we had spoken he rang Lennon back and said, 'I've rethought it and I've gone to this other person. I think you should do the same because I'm not happy about my introduction of Klein.' But it was too late.

I met Allen Klein in London during the early days of working through the Stones' documents. I had to be extremely careful with him because I was well aware that everybody around me thought that I was getting into a situation where the risk was greater than the potential reward.

Klein was equally careful with me. He was very wary indeed, and I think that shortly after we met he realised that in some way or other he, too, was at risk. He came across as oily, but at the same time aggressive. I soon realised that with anything he said, there was no reason why one should either believe or disbelieve it.

Mick found it a lot harder to deal directly with Allen Klein. He felt very aggrieved, that Klein had acted improperly, and that he, Mick, had been made to look a fool. There was one frightening incident in the Savoy Hotel when Mick started screaming at Klein who darted out of the room and ran down the corridor with Mick in hot pursuit. I had to stop him and say, 'You cannot risk laying a hand on Klein.' In retrospect I thought it was probably a good idea that Keith had not joined us on that occasion.

Essentially the band were handcuffed on the one side by their contract with Allen Klein and on the other to Decca Records, and my job was going to be to allow them to escape, Houdini-like, from both with the minimum damage. There was no question of renegotiating the contract with Decca. The challenge was how to get out of that contract, because they had no freedom to go to any other record company. Decca had rights over works 'created in whole or in part'. There was hardly any room for manoeuvre.

However, the contract with Decca was completely normal. What was abnormal was the contract they had with Klein, as we discovered in due course.

Having read about the Beatles and Northern Songs, and how they had made a substantial amount of money selling the copyrights in their songs, which clearly had a value, and after giving careful thought to the tax implications, I decided that examining the Stones' financial affairs would be ideal work for an intelligent set of financial advisers, which essentially is what Leopold Joseph was.

I also realised that if a way could be found to get through and past the lack of transparency and the dodgy business practices which surrounded the touring business, there was a lot of money to be made, although at the time the artists were making no money out of touring.

However, it seemed obvious that the artists who could make money were the ones who performed well. And I had seen enough of Mick and the Stones to realise that performance was their forte. The potential for money was there. It was not going to disappear. The trick would be to make sure the money went to the performers, not the promoters. I resolved to tackle that issue as soon as the immediate knotty legal issues were resolved.

The group's documents arrived – in truckloads. I persuaded my colleagues and company lawyers to look at all the documents for no charge. This, I have always thought, was one of the most remarkable deals I have ever negotiated.

At this stage my contact with the Stones was with Mick, acting on behalf of the group. The rest of the band would not have wanted to be involved. They rarely had anything to do with the business side. I met the others and we all understood each other, since they were very pleased with what I was doing on their behalf. However, even though Keith lived just down the road from Mick at 3 Cheyne Walk, I did not meet him for quite a few months after I had started analysing the situation.

In fact, since I was always keen to do these things in what I thought was the correct way, I had asked each of the others to come to my office, but I could not get Keith for months. This disturbed me. I got rather annoyed and wrote him a stiff letter, essentially saying, 'Since I gather the intention is that we should be working together, I think it is important to meet.'

Finally he did turn up, and I was as impressed by him as I had been with Mick, though in a completely different way. I had an intuition about Keith, which I might have been hard pressed to articulate at the time.

I saw that Keith was in a way – and I hesitate to say this – the most intelligent mind of all the band. Certainly he had an aura about him, like Mick a *je ne sais quoi* that would be exhilarating to be involved in. His aura to me was that of generations of travelling circus folk, like Sleary's Circus in Dickens' *Hard Times*: entertainers but also with something of the pilgrim.

The other band members made less impact on me. Bill Wyman struck me as a perfectly normal, rather ordinary young man. In the early stages I thought – wrongly – that he had a certain financial intellect and wanted him to take on the role of the financial scribe within the group. I hoped he would become the Stones' calculating machine so that our

My mother, Countess Bianca Henriette Maria Fischler von Treuberg – a friend described her as 'very tall and stately with ice-blue eyes'.

My father, Prince Leopold zu Loewenstein-Wertheim-Freudenberg. 'No woman married to a Loewenstein', he once wrote, 'can for long live outside history.'

Schloss Holzen, my mother's family home between Augsburg and Munich. Due to my grandfather's financial extravagance, it was sold off to Franciscan nuns before I was born.

My parents in a rare photograph of them as a couple. They did not stay together for long, although long enough to produce me.

With my mother in Europe in 1939: I spent the early months of the War in France before being flown out on one of the last civilian flights before Paris fell.

Aged 16: after school at St Christopher's in Letchworth, I prepared for my Oxford entrance examination with tutors in Cambridge.

Dancing with Miss Julie de Pentheny O'Kelly at the coming-out dance for Anne Charleton at Londonderry House on Park Lane, July 1950.

An informal portrait of Josephine, née Lowry-Corry, shortly before we were married.

Josephine photographed by Antony Armstrong-Jones before he married Princess Margaret and was created 1st Earl of Snowdon.

Emerging from our wedding in July 1957 at the Brompton Oratory in South Kensington. Forty-one years later our daughter Dora was married in the same church.

Josephine with our sons Konrad and Rudolf.

In stern financier mode: I became managing director of the merchant bank Leopold Joseph in 1963, shortly before my thirtieth birthday.

Some time away from the demands and unsociable timetables of the international financial markets, with Josephine and the boys in the garden at Holland Villas Road.

Josephine in Venice – a regular destination for us through the years. Our son Konrad is now priest at the eighteenth-century church San Simeon Piccolo in Santa Croce.

On an Italian adventure with Peter Sellers and Britt Ekland, and (*sitting*) Dino Pecci-Blunt, Circeo, May 1965.

Attending Baron Alexis de Redé's grand Oriental Ball at the Hotel Lambert in Paris, December 1969. I am wearing a costume based on a Léon Bakst design; Josephine's was her own design.

Guests at the White Ball we held in
Holland Villas Road in July 1969: Cecil
Beaton and HRH Princess Margaret with
(*seated*) Deborah, Duchess of Devonshire;
Peter Sellers and Miranda Quarry;
Marianne Faithfull; Mick Jagger with
Cecil Beaton and Marianne; Christopher
Gibbs and Lindy Dufferin.

Hosting the White Ball: Josephine in a lace trouser suit, my white patent leather shoes garnished with gold buckles. The décor for the party was masterminded by David Mlinaric.

discussions would be more straightforward, but I soon saw that was not possible.

Charlie Watts was diffident, charming, basically a nice man with a strong artistic talent, with his jazz and his draughtsmanship. Mick Taylor was good-looking in a conventional way, which none of the others were. He had been brought in to replace Brian Jones, whose death had somewhat complicated matters from my point of view, because all the contracts involved him. Consequently I had to deal with the solicitor looking after the Stones' affairs, Guy Berger, a good, honest man but who was somewhat out of his area of expertise since he had no experience or understanding of what we now call the rock business (but which in those days we wouldn't have known what to call).

I looked for a firm of solicitors who would understand the business. I was doing some work for the publisher George Weidenfeld at the time, and I discussed with him which lawyers he thought might be appropriate. He recommended a Hungarian lawyer, a senior partner at Theodore Goddard, who at once grasped the issues, but said, 'I'm not the right partner to deal with this, but I do have two fellow partners who are both excellent, one for commercial undertakings, and the other on tax matters.'

The first stage of my involvement was a question of analysing the Stones' contracts, by going through every single document, which I did with the assistance of the two partners at Theodore Goddard. After reviewing a few of the basic documents I realised why the Stones would not have received the money which Mick had questioned at our first meeting. It would have gone to Klein and therefore they would have depended on what *he* gave them, as opposed to what the record company or the publishing company did. They were completely in the hands of a man who was like an old-fashioned Indian moneylender, in other words somebody who takes everything and only releases to others a tiny sliver of income, before tax . . .

There were, not surprisingly, no statements of accounts from Allen Klein. The only way to work out what had gone to whom was by meticulously going through all the computations which were included in the mass of papers that their old solicitors and accountants possessed. Of course, they had reviewed all the papers that they received from Decca and from Andrew Oldham and ticked them. One had to realise that they had never been truly informed as to the risks that they'd be running as the creditors of a buccaneering American accountant.

The role of the band's previous advisers was not an issue. They simply were not aware either of the potential profits that the Rolling Stones could generate or the abnormality of the contracts that they had signed with Decca, Oldham and Klein.

It took eighteen months, indeed until 1970 when the Stones' existing contracts came to an end, to work through the stacks of papers. The contracts for the recording and publishing of the Stones' music would have to be renegotiated, debts repaid pursuant to the Allen Klein agreements, and money had to be found for the tax they owed – 83–98 per cent on their income – and for which no provision had been made.

As I took stock of the evidence from reading all the documentation and papers, and from what I had learnt and understood of the overall situation, I now had to decide how to resolve what was clearly a rats' nest of complications, and how to untangle the relationship between the Stones and Decca, and between the Stones and Allen Klein. Otherwise forward progress was going to be impossible.

During all of this time I was working, and working hard. Analysing the Stones' financial situation was highly detailed, painstaking, fastidious work and for me somewhat uncharted territory. In the days before word processors, faxes and e-mails, documents had to be typed from the start and then retyped again and again. Indeed, even this does not encompass the fact that many different documents had to be sifted apart so that the real basis of what the Stones had made and what the manager had taken could be shown.

But I had found something that interested me and that was the lawsuits. Perhaps because I possessed the mind of a lawyer, even if I had never entered the profession, it amused me to see what one could do and what one couldn't do and whether the lawyers made sense or whether they didn't.

Many years later we found ourselves staying as guests in the house near Grasse belonging to our friend Tom Parr, a decorator (which he preferred to the term 'interior designer') who had set up a partnership with David Hicks before joining Colefax and Fowler. Herbert von Karajan's man of business was there for lunch, and I remember saying to Josephine, 'Ah, how I wish that I had his job, and he had mine. I would be so much happier looking after Karajan than rock stars.' Josephine tartly replied that I was quite wrong, 'Nonsense. You would mind if Karajan had a bad performance, but you couldn't care less if now and then they perform badly. It is far easier for you not to be involved except for keeping an eye to see that they follow their new guidelines, rather than getting upset if they goof onstage.' It was a perceptive remark of hers, and quite true.

To progress the situation for the Stones, I had to find both American and English lawyers to work with since much of the business with Allen Klein had been carried out under American law. The bulk of the significant recording documents were with London Records, the US subsidiary of Decca. Simultaneously we were having to deal not only with our solicitors in London for the contract with Decca itself but also with both the American and British lawyers for the Stones' relationship with Klein, London Records and the various publishing issues.

Going shopping for lawyers in New York I found hilariously funny. I had been given a number of names of large law firms in the city. As I contacted each of them I realised that this must represent an important piece of future business for them. Although I was new to the entertainment industry, I was not being put off by any of the law firms and all the meetings that were set up were with their most senior partners. Perhaps I may be being a little naïve about myself. I think the Americans were amused, maybe even amazed, to meet somebody with a name like mine, and therefore were interested to see what on earth this strange person was like.

In my own way I imagine I was as alien a being to them as the Stones initially were to me. Many people I came across were completely thrown by how they should address me. Over the years Josephine collected some excellent examples of misspellings and wayward appellations, which she would swap with Deborah, Duchess of Devonshire. One I particularly recall was being dubbed 'the Orince', which my son Konrad thereafter used to call me for many a long year.

However, my unusual appellation was not the sole reason. I soon understood that the primary reason those senior partners were keen to arrange meetings with me was because they knew that there was money to be made in this field. Which, at the time, the British did *not* realise. Even the stuffiest of New York's lawyers did not want to turn down something which might prove to be a major source of income – and a few of the very bright ones were convinced that it would happen.

Popular music has always made a lot of money in America; the lawyers were well aware of the amounts of money involved and thought that a large chunk of that really ought to come to them. Whereas the English lawyers – who were paying the vast rate of tax in force at the time – could not be bothered to become involved with something which they considered not at all lucrative and therefore unduly troublesome.

This brings one to an important distinction between American and British lawyers. British lawyers at the time certainly would never have tried to be managers and involve themselves in taking a role which they were not trained for or not able to do, whereas in America lawyers, like the Eastmans, were already taking on those responsibilities.

The American lawyers were far more aware of the realities of the music industry, and hence keen to work with us. Most of them would have been happy to take on the work involved, but to employ them would have cost the Stones a vast amount of money.

In London at the time even senior partners could not charge much more than £50 an hour (in 1969 figures), whereas the American firms would have put five partners on the job each charging an average of $500 a day, plus expenses. If one had gone to the American equivalent of leading law firms like Freshfields or Slaughter and May, they would have put batteries of lawyers on it and the expenses would have been astronomical.

I realised that one had to be particularly careful with

American lawyers because the list of lawyers whom one thought of as the best were prohibitively expensive, whereas those who were smaller and the ones who had music industry talents were at least available at an affordable rate.

Meanwhile, my partners in Leopold Joseph were rightly concerned as I appeared to be spending all my time on the work with the Stones with no charge. I was not even charging for the very frequent, and costly, trips to America which took up a lot of my time. It was all pure outgoings, with nothing to show on the income side – and in the event I was not able to send a bill to the Stones until 1972, three years after actively starting work on their affairs.

Despite the complications of the contractual arrangements, nonetheless I remained intrigued by the whole situation. My gut feeling was that in the end I would be able to prevail. Just as in a game of chess when at any given point the next move may determine whether you are going to win or lose, I could look ahead and see how the pieces might be moved successfully.

I did not think that we were necessarily going to make a huge amount of money, but I did think I was going to gain the Stones their liberty from Decca and therefore that they would be free to negotiate a new contract, which was key. Moreover, I believed that Leopold Joseph would secure a reasonable fee from the future earnings of the masters and the copyrights which the Stones had sold – most disadvantageously – to Allen Klein.

As far as the past earnings were concerned I knew there was a risk that I might not be able to achieve any improvement, since it was clear that when the Stones had signed the bewildering mass of contracts they had been represented and advised by lawyers and that, as the old American saying had it, they were 'free, white and twenty-one', in other words masters of their own destiny, free to do as they pleased. I knew from the very early days of our investigations that this was the case. That knowledge, which was very depressing, was the advantage of having read every one of those seemingly endless documents. But it also made it clear that new commissions could be made for work they had not yet done during the early contract period.

How much money could be received from taking a larger share of what came in to Klein's companies depended on what the final summing-up would be by the lawyers and the arbitrator. I had settled on the law firm run by Harold Orenstein, an entertainment lawyer who had done extensive work in the area of copyright law, especially with the Broadway composer Frank Loesser. Harold Orenstein and his partner had just hired a bright young litigator, Peter Parcher, who in turn found us a first-class arbitrator, Lloyd Cutler, a senior partner of an extremely powerful Washington firm. Allen Klein had nominated as his lawyer Max Freund, of a well-known firm, who was an excellent, indeed fearsome, opponent. The legal battle would be long.

The shadow falling over my ability to negotiate a good deal was if Klein's arbitrators could show that the Stones had not been forthright about the work that they had 'in whole or in part' performed during the period that they had signed up with Klein. This came to light for us when the arbitration had already started.

To extract the band from Decca required delicate negotiations. Decca were as unhappy with the Stones as the band were with Decca. The head of Decca was Sir Edward Lewis, an Establishment figure who had played an important role with radar during the war. He viewed the Rolling Stones with the same distaste as my partners in Leopold Joseph. Decca were amazed that the group sold so many records. The company did not understand rock music. Having famously turned down the Beatles and allowed them to be signed by EMI, though, they had been determined not to miss out on the Stones.

Against this the Stones did not see why they had to explain their position, or even discuss what songs they might or might not have written while under contract to Decca. They believed they had a God-given gift to write songs which people liked to listen to and watch being performed, and how dare other people have any title whatsoever to their craft? I and the lawyers had to point out that whatever their emotional feelings about that craft, they were in terms of the law wrong, and that the law alas was right.

The documents covering their publishing deal stated that the Rolling Stones were tied up for their copyrights covering all the work they had done, or *had started but not finished*. This latter was the critical point as any demos or half-finished scraps of songs would be considered to fall under the existing deal.

We were dealing with Mr Rowe of Rowe and Moore representing Decca: established, old-fashioned solicitors, very bright. The early meetings were difficult, because they resisted very strongly having to show their documents to anybody else. I wrote many letters to Mr Rowe to which he never replied.

The specialist tax lawyer at Theodore Goddard, a Mrs Stacey, was absolutely brilliant, and she accompanied me to a meeting with Rowe and Moore. I asked Mr Rowe, 'One thing has always disturbed me. Why did you never answer these letters?' 'Mrs Stacey will inform you,' he said, 'that we are not legally bound to answer your letters.' The prospect of a resolution looked unlikely.

This was exacerbated when the band's friend Marshall Chess – from the Chess Records family in Chicago – came to a meeting at Decca with Sir Edward Lewis. Sir Edward asked Marshall Chess, 'I imagine you know the details of the state of the work the Rolling Stones were doing.' 'Oh yes,' said Marshall. 'You've got the complete list.' As we walked back across the bridge opposite the Decca building following the meeting, Marshall suddenly started hooting with laughter. 'There's a huge amount of songs we've not talked about!'

Mrs Stacey and I were horrified. We had to ring Mick and the others and spell out in no uncertain terms that all of the negotiations would have to be changed because we would have to go back to Decca and tell them there was more unfinished work, in which they had rights. It also made the litigation with Allen Klein even harder.

During the British revenue case, when the group's earnings were under scrutiny, the Revenue's very able litigator thought he saw the basis for a large contractual sum due to the Stones on which they had not been taxed. My answer to this was that I much admired the Revenue's meticulous examination of the records but that the Stones themselves and their lawyers' accountants had also tried to find this sum but to no avail!

It was not easy to see where one could have changed things. The Inland Revenue performed a special audit, and they were equally mystified by all the contracts that they had seen and believed that there must have been more money involved.

I remember appearing before the Revenue enquiry, and

having to give evidence. The prosecutor for the Inland Revenue was a very civil man, who said, 'Well, there's all the money that was paid by the publishing, they must have got that, surely this contract allows for it?' I answered, 'No, I can assure you that I've looked at that matter very, very carefully and I was as amazed as you are to find no money had arisen from it. Oddly enough I and the Revenue are as one on this matter, and I only wish you had asked Mr Klein what it means.'

There was laughter in court, but it was a very serious matter. Not only did the Stones have no money, but they were in danger of being sued by the Inland Revenue and put, as it were, in the spiritual equivalent of the Marshalsea, the old debtors' prison in Southwark made famous by Dickens, whose father had been sent there.

What had also become apparent to me was that the band would have to abandon their UK residence. If they did not do this, they could be paying between 83 and 98 per cent of their profits in British income tax and surtax.

Mick had appeared as an actor in Nick Roeg's film *Performance* and was now out on location in Australia, having been signed up to act in the title role of Tony Richardson's *Ned Kelly*.

Mick called me from Australia and asked me, 'What shall we do?' I had reached a critical juncture. A week or so before I had explained what I had uncovered, that there would be long and unpleasant litigation to go through in order to extricate the band from the various contracts. This in itself would entail three sets of fees, the American lawyers', the British lawyers' and my own. It was a difficult decision for him to make, and he felt nervous about making the plunge. However, I now needed him to decide, as, if he did not wish to take my advice, I would have to walk away and leave him to sort out the mess alone.

'My advice is contained in four words,' I told him. 'Drop Klein and out.' By 'out' I meant 'leave the country'. Mick had been unwilling to make a break with Allen Klein until he knew what was going to happen. But now I had to underscore that there was simply no choice. 'Drop Klein and out. You've got to do that. You must either say yes or no.' He said, 'Yes', and so everything started from there.

Once the decision had been made to move out of the country for tax reasons, we had to find a suitable location. I felt strongly that it should not be far away. The Stones always struck me as a very English band, and, despite Mick and Keith's recent trip to Brazil, I did not think anywhere too far-flung would suit them.

I selected the South of France for that very reason: it was the easiest place for English people to go. I had thought of all the places where, taxwise, it would be convenient, certainly Ireland, also Holland, Sweden, Denmark, Germany, Italy. Ireland might have been suitable as a destination, but I felt not as sure taxwise, nor was I convinced that living there would be sufficient to overcome the residency requirements. And it was far too early to contemplate the band settling in America. It would never have worked.

There were a number of reasons why I thought the South of France would be appropriate. I knew the region very well from my childhood and had spent much time there subsequently.

After settling on France, I worked hard through my connections to organise a suitable place to live. To assist me in that, I consulted the senior French lawyer Maître Jean Michard-Pellissier and asked him to negotiate the French tax position.

There were two well-known international lawyers in Paris at this time, the brilliant René de Chambrun (a descendant of Lafayette who married Pierre Laval's daughter Josée), and the equally talented Michard-Pellissier.

Alexis de Redé had introduced me to Maître Michard-Pellissier. He was a close friend of the Prime Minister Jacques Chaban-Delmas, and had been the lawyer for Henri Charrière, of *Papillon* fame. I had used him on some earlier business deals, and he seemed ideal for the delicate negotiations required to come to an arrangement to define the financial basis with the authorities in the *département* of the Alpes-Maritimes; there was a lot of work to be done behind the scenes so that the artists could live in comfort in a foreign country.

Maître Michard-Pellissier dealt directly with the *préfet* for the Alpes-Maritimes. A deal was struck with the Alpes-Maritimes authorities whereby the Stones were allowed to reside and only had to pay a negotiated income tax (this arrangement later blew up when the drug problems reared their ugly head with Keith and Anita, and we had to hold extraordinary meetings, like something from a Fernandel farce, with the authorities and the police in Nice).

By and large the South of France was the right place because we knew people on whom we could rely regarding the taxation side. In those days, full exchange controls existed and it was most important to have this sorted out at the beginning of their residence if they later wished to leave.

Sam White, the *Evening Standard*'s Paris correspondent, broke the story in October 1970. 'The Rolling Stones, I understand, are discussing a plan to emigrate to France – physically and financially. The whole move is rightly shrouded in the kind of secrecy reserved for major financial operations.'

Once we had made the decision to decamp to France, I had people who could look for houses and villas for each of the band. They, sometimes with the Stones' various girlfriends and wives, or their secretaries, went on reconnaissance visits, to draw up a shortlist of suitable properties.

Charlie Watts still has the house he bought then, and Bill Wyman kept his for a long time. I told all the band that they should buy the houses freehold. Charlie and Bill listened to my advice, but unfortunately Mick and Keith chose not to. Mick decided not to buy a house, which in retrospect was short-sighted. Keith could have converted the rental deal he had on the house that he and Anita chose – the fabulous Nellcôte, high up above the bay at Villefranche – into a purchase but never did. At that stage the property might have been available for no more than £30,000 or £40,000.

With the assistance of the band's mobile recording van, which had driven down from London, Nellcôte became the location for the recording of the next Stones album.

I spent that period flying down to Nice on a regular basis – in those days flying was still a pleasure – and heading up to see the band from my hotel to discuss ongoing matters.

On one trip as I was about to leave Nice Airport, and was with Mick and Keith and one or two of the others, I suddenly looked at the French police in the way that the Stones must always have looked at them. I had always naturally viewed the police as people who would be there to help one if there was any unpleasantness and to keep the drug pushers away. But suddenly I saw them through Mick and Keith's eyes as a threatening presence and I realised how appalling that might become.

When I needed to see the group, I saw them. Alan Dunn,

Mick's Leporello, and the other personal assistants always arranged the time for our meetings, and made sure that the band members would be available. I was there for business. I had no interest in going down to the makeshift studio in the basement of Nellcôte, where the sessions for the new album were rumbling on.

That new album in due course became *Exile On Main Street*, which may be one of the few top-selling albums, if not the only one, to contain a reference to tax planning in the title.

6

'Life is all memory, except for the one present moment that goes by you so quickly you hardly catch it going.'

Tennessee Williams

Very early on, because of Allen Klein on the one hand and Ahmet Ertegun on the other, I spent a great deal of time travelling to America, attempting to disentangle the Stones from Klein and to *entangle* them with Ahmet's company, Atlantic Records. As the Stones' existing contracts drew to an end in 1970–71 there was an increasing urgency to clarify our rights and a definition of what, if any, ABKCO and Decca Records would still possess.

It was Ahmet Ertegun who really precipitated the time constraints. The band had recorded the best part of what was going to be their first record for him and Atlantic Records, and Ahmet was keen on releasing it. Since Atlantic had advanced some money for that record, which would eventually be *Sticky Fingers*, we had to come to a compromise with Allen Klein and Decca to know what, if anything, were their rights on masters and copyrights. As can be imagined, this affected us in many ways. I thought to myself that a really shrewd man like Ahmet was not going to be keen, really keen, to make friends with all of us unless he could see genuine potential.

I had first met Ahmet Ertegun at a dinner party given by the fashion designer Hardy Amies. Driving home I said to Josephine, 'I was so pleased to meet Ahmet.' And she asked, 'Are you talking about the man with the beard?' 'Yes.' She said, 'I thought your interest and the fact that you were talking to him so much was that you thought he was an Öttingen', who are an important Bavarian princely family. And I said, 'No he's not an Öttingen, he's an Ertegun, a Turk in New York', whose father had been sent by Mustafa Kemal Atatürk in 1935 to be the first ambassador to the United States for the recently created Republic of Turkey.

Ahmet Ertegun was one of the few people that one could say had a happy life. Most people encounter some major problem in their life which they have to overcome. Some succeed, some do not. Ahmet was always happy, cheerful and perfectly in keeping with the American concepts that everybody can try and do something for themselves, and that you never know whether you are going to succeed, but it's worth the risk.

To start the company, Ahmet had borrowed $10,000 from his family dentist and launched Atlantic Records in 1947 as a label initially concentrating on R&B and jazz. Atlantic proved to be extremely successful; Ahmet made a lot of friends and a lot of money. And he deserved both.

When I first talked to Mick he told me that he and the rest of the band had met Ahmet Ertegun and that Atlantic could be an interesting company for them to sign to, especially as it was an American rather than a British company. Of course, I was delighted to hear this because it would provide an additional reason for them to leave England.

After meeting Ahmet we set about working out the contractual details. Having a record company in place, who were extremely helpful, was a great advantage and from my own point of view I learnt a great deal from my involvement in so many lawsuits. Atlantic Records and all their lawyers were only too pleased to help me and teach me what was normal, and not normal, record industry practice. It was the steepest of learning curves, and an extremely good training that would stand me in very good stead in the years to come.

What none of us anticipated was that we would be engaged in litigation for the next eighteen years. I had thought it might take perhaps three or four years to work through all the contractual problems. Allen Klein had, of course, worked out that from his point of view the longer everything dragged on the better, and he knew that he could make difficulties both by not paying the royalties that were due to the Stones and by saying that certain masters and copyrights belonged to him.

One of my problems was that I was not able to send the Stones a bill for my time until an initial settlement with Allen Klein was achieved, agreed and signed off, and any cash due was paid over to the band by Klein. I was working very hard to achieve that, and I was still working for Leopold Joseph. My partners in the bank were saying, perfectly reasonably, 'Rupert, you cannot spend all your time working on this, and travelling to America, if you don't get our fees paid.' However, if there was a chance that we would ever receive any money, I had to see to it that the Stones received at least some of the money from royalties and earnings to which we believed they were entitled, but this was entirely dependent on reaching a settlement with Klein.

In those early days there was a risk that there would never be any money. I knew that Atlantic would be putting out the next record, and so, as was usual with them, they paid for the expenses of managers while they were in America: the cost of cars and taxis would be covered, but the hotel bills and the travel to and from the States were all being paid for by Leopold Joseph.

Ahmet Ertegun made two valuable contributions to our ongoing battle with Klein. He made the point to Allen Klein that he, Ahmet, was there, that he was going to fund the Stones and that in his view it would be far better for Klein to leave gracefully rather than stir up an enormous amount of fuss. Ahmet also introduced me to an attorney, Mickey Rubin, Frank Sinatra's lawyer. But even with Mickey Rubin's involvement, the litigation crept painfully forwards.

Fortunately I managed to negotiate a satisfactory contract with Allen Klein at the end of a meeting in May 1972. This took place in the offices of our New York lawyers on Broadway, started in the late afternoon and finished at breakfast the next day.

I recently discovered, among the boxes and cartons of papers related to the Klein litigation, a paper I had prepared as a detailed briefing document a couple of months in advance: twelve pages of analysis on tightly typed foolscap paper which I entitled 'Prolegomena on ABKCO/Stones Settlement'.

'We are not all that far apart on settlement terms,' I wrote. 'It is therefore consequently feasible that a settlement may be reached but further pressure may have to be applied.' That pressure could, I suggested, come from the Stones themselves and perhaps Atlantic, pointing out that Klein's ability to keep his clients, let alone to get new ones, would be severely endangered even if he won the lawsuit, since the case would disclose exactly how much profit he was taking for himself.

During the negotiations that May evening Mick and Keith went out and had dinner and brought back some dancing girls into these very correct lawyers' offices where the negotiations were underway. This vastly lightened the proceedings.

I was installed in one of the offices with Allen Klein and our respective key lawyers, with further lawyers in other offices waiting to be called in as required. Occasionally the noise of the party and all the fun that Mick, Keith and the girls were having wafted in from the room that they had commandeered. During the course of the evening Ahmet Ertegun dropped by and chatted to us all. Robert Frank, who was filming a documentary (which later emerged as *Cocksucker Blues*), was also part of the entourage swirling around the detailed, delicate, intensive and important discussions I was trying to guide to a conclusion.

At one point Allen Klein and I were left alone. He immediately started rifling through the drawers of a desk and found an internal memo itemising the fees that the partner was going to charge us. He was absolutely delighted by this discovery, and made a point of showing me those charges he thought were particularly juicy. It was typical of his cheek and bravado. We never became friends – the matters we were arguing over were far too serious and antagonistic for that – but we established a strange kind of rapport over the years of our seemingly endless legal wrangles.

At eight in the morning we reached an agreement. I went out to have breakfast at my hotel with Diego Del Vayo – the son of the Spanish Republic's foreign minister in the 1930s, and one of the most amusing people I have met. At one of Ahmet and his wife Mica's parties Diego, a stockbroker, was talking about various shares and the state of the market. Ahmet said, 'Stop talking about these stocks and shares. I invested $20,000 in a stock you were pushing three weeks ago, called Liquidometer, and I realised you had sold the shares at a loss of $15,000. Call that good stockbroking?' Diego pushed up his glasses, and replied, 'Ahmet, please remember that I lost much more money for people that I like!'

So Diego and I headed off for breakfast where both Mick and Keith joined us. The breakfast lasted a good couple of hours. We were in celebratory mood, because, although we had had to make a few concessions, the key result was that we had got some money. I had set myself the goal of extracting one million dollars from Klein's pocket and we had come away with more.

The key objective had been satisfactorily dealt with. The Rolling Stones were now free to record for a company of their choice and the sum they obtained would be greater than their old contractual commissions which had been withheld pending negotiations. They did not preclude us from future litigation since Klein found point after point of increasing triviality which had to be put before the New York courts and the federal courts. In the case against them and the Inland Revenue there were law suits spread over seventeen years.

In general I have kept my friends separate from the people I do business with, but from the outset Ahmet Ertegun and I got on very well and we became great friends. Josephine was equally fond of him and we sought out each other's company whenever we were in the same place. We stayed with Ahmet and Mica at their houses in New York, at Southampton on Long Island, and at Bodrum in Turkey. He had also taken a house for several years in Barbados which we often visited, and from there we would often fly over by small plane to see Mustique, which also became a regular part of our lives.

The island of Mustique had been bought in the early 1960s by Colin Tennant, a cousin of Josephine's and the brother of James, who gave the dinner where Josephine and I first properly met. Colin spent a substantial amount of money developing the infrastructure of the island and by presenting one of the houses to Princess Margaret, as a wedding present, took a significant step in making Mustique an amusing and entertaining spot.

In the first years Mustique was really like Bembridge in the Caribbean. English people who would previously have gone to the Isle of Wight found themselves constructing the same kind of rather rickety houses as they would have built by the English seashore, and the island developed the feel of a holiday village either on the South Coast or in Normandy. Many of the houses were designed by Oliver Messel (Lord Snowdon's uncle) with a Caribbean flavour.

Apart from the English backbone of Mustique's residents many Venezuelans came because the island is only 250 miles from Caracas. It would only take them two hours to get from Caracas to Mustique by plane, which was probably less time than driving to their ranch from the city.

Colin had worked out a treaty with the government of St Vincent and the Grenadines and had managed to put into place a very good agreement which included a tax-free status for new residents, which was one of the reasons that people went there: it was a favourable offshore centre, dependent on

Barbados and St Vincent, large islands still belonging to the UK, which had their own regime.

As I continued to think about the tax status of the Stones, I had realised that they had to gain non-resident status, since that was the only way they could ever dream of being able to pay off their taxes.

At the time, to be considered as non-resident it was generally thought that you were obliged to spend no more than ninety days a year in England for three years with an additional absence of one complete year, and not to have a house or housing registered in your name in the UK.

Keith did not really want his life to be bothered by matters such as tax, and only reluctantly agreed to become a non-resident, although he enjoyed himself tremendously once he had done so. However, Mustique was not the right place for him, whereas I was able to persuade Mick to buy a place there quite soon after we had started working together.

He still has the same residence, though it is now much enlarged and enhanced, and very well looked after. Josephine and I were also regular visitors to the island. By and large we knew everybody who went there, whereas now that is no longer the case. Initially we stayed as guests of Colin Tennant's, and then rented houses there. Only as late as 1998 did we decide to buy a property on the island. As we already had a house in London and another in Los Angeles I was much opposed to having one anywhere else, particularly since it was a maxim of Josephine's that one should never have more than two houses. However, having decided to break her own rule, she spent twenty years trying to get me to agree to have a house in Mustique, while I stoutly resisted. Having finally been persuaded, the result was that, as usual, she was right and I was wrong.

We spent a great deal of time finding the right place and followed the advice of a friend: 'For goodness' sake don't buy a house in an untreated area because it may be years before electricity and the other services are installed. It is much better for you to buy something, pull it down and put it up again.' This was excellent advice and is precisely what we did.

We bought an existing house, pulled down the centre block which was unfinished, and based the rebuilding on an Oliver Messel design. Originally called 'Banana Bread', we renamed it 'Zinnia'. Josephine has created a very pretty house adorned with enchanting murals by a young Irishman, Michael Dillon, whose father commanded the Life Guards.

As we had found during all our stays on Mustique, until the arrival of the mobile phone one was relatively out of touch except for things which were very important. It was a good place to recharge one's batteries. And if Mick happened to be there at the same time we were able to talk together and discuss issues in a relaxed, stress-free environment. I suspect not many recording artists and their business managers had the opportunity to use that kind of escape valve at that time.

In the meantime I was exploring the ways in which my pre-Stones life could be valuable to my work with the band. I always used any contacts I had in place to work closely with the British Embassy or consular staff in any country where the Stones were touring. This first became important in 1972 when the band wanted to go to Japan, and Japan refused to give them visas. It happened that I knew the ambassador, Sir Fred Warner. Although older than I was, he had also been to Magdalen and had recently been appointed to the post in Tokyo, at a time when Japan was emerging as a potent economic force.

I rang him and explained the problem; he told me he would see what could be done. When he rang back he said that indeed there was a problem. 'Would it help,' I asked, 'if I could discuss it with you in person?' Yes, he said, come and stay. So I went over to Tokyo and stayed at the Embassy where, in talking things over, I learnt that Fred had found out that the ban was because of the drugs raid at Mick's house in Cheyne Walk in May 1969.

In the end we managed to provide evidence that there was controversy concerning the reliability of that particular bust but I thought to myself that we should never again find ourselves in a similar situation, and I always saw to it that, if I did not already know the ambassador in a particular country, I always knew somebody who did. I would arrange that the Stones were invited to a reception at the Embassy, and for the ambassador and his wife and the staff to have tickets for the shows, which they were delighted to receive. By making such strong links – and I am sure that no other rock band at the time would have gone anywhere remotely near the British Embassy unless under duress – we had an ally if and when anything went wrong.

I started looking at other opportunities for the band to perform further afield. The Stones were anxious to see whether they could play in the USSR. They knew that their records were being played there – for which they received no royalties, of course – and like all of us were fascinated to see what the country was like. So I thought that it was worth going there to see if it would be feasible.

My mother knew a charming and extremely entertaining old Russian who went by the name of George St George. He always said, 'I am no more called George St George than I am called Marilyn Monroe, but I was born in Siberia where all the nicest Russians come from.' I believe that his forebears had been Decembrists in the uprising of 1825 and had been moved to Siberia where they had a large estate and a comfortable life.

Kissed as a child by Lenin, George had later been involved in helping both Russia and America during the later stages of the Second World War. He explained to me that Russia and Japan did not go to war until the very end, when Stalin, as can be expected, wanted to pick up some profits from being the victor in the war against Germany. George proved to be very useful to Russia and to America via Japan because Russia needed rubber and Japan needed steel, so he entered into a complicated switch arrangement whereby this was provided.

George was of immense help when I travelled to Russia in 1973 to open discussions. The critical element was to have a conference with the cultural department of the Russian government. When we arrived in Moscow, we stayed at the historic Hotel National, where Josephine and I had a suite with a vast drawing room and a grand piano which she was very keen to play on since, by and large, she used to practise the piano every day. Opening the keyboard lid she saw that there were no keys and on further investigation no strings either. It just looked grand.

Before going I had had a long chat with Diana Vreeland, who had been over to Russia to organise an exhibition of the Metropolitan Museum of Art's collection of costumes in the Hermitage. She said, 'You'll enjoy it very much.' 'And what's your greatest tip for us?' 'Tip,' she said. George St George told us 'Bring cowrie shells, bring cigarettes, bring LPs, and you'll find you have a very enjoyable time.'

George had a great friend who was in the Supreme Soviet, the poet, author and translator Sergei Michalkov, who was then the head of the Cultural Sub-Ministry. He had been commissioned by Stalin to write the lyrics for the Russian national anthem – and subsequently had to rework them following Stalin's death to remove any reference to the former leader. In 2001 Vladimir Putin asked him, then in his eighties, to rewrite the words one more time.

Josephine and I were at dinner in the Hotel National. We had ordered our food but nothing had arrived. Suddenly a hush came over the restaurant, in a way one was only used to seeing in England when a member of the royal family entered a room. We looked up and saw a very good-looking grey-haired man of about six foot three. This was none other than George's friend Sergei Michalkov. He came over and asked if everything was all right. Josephine said, 'Well, we've been waiting for our chicken, and they have just told us after half an hour that there is no chicken.' Michalkov lifted a finger. The head waiter scuttled up to him. 'Chicken – *at once*,' Michalkov ordered. The chicken duly appeared – at once!

I later asked Michalkov about the fact that it appeared to me that many of the police we saw in Red Square were high-ranking, decorated officers. He answered, 'Of course. You would not want Somebodies to be arrested by Nobodies.'

On one occasion we had gone out to Michalkov's dacha for a party where a cellist played one of Benjamin Britten's cello suites for us after lunch. While we were chatting over tea, I pointed to the portrait of a pretty lady that clearly dated from before the Revolution. Who was it? I asked. 'That is my grandmother. She was a Princess Galitzine.' 'I didn't realise,' I said, 'that there were many former members of the aristocracy in the Supreme Soviet.' 'Oh yes, there are a few of us, though Gagarin was not,' he replied. 'There is a lot of rubbish thought about the Soviet Union in the West. We have a peaceful and tranquil society without murders or robberies and people can bring their children up safely. Periodically there are minor insurrections, but thank God we have the KGB and can usually stop them.'

Nearly thirty years later, in 1998, when we saw Sergei in Moscow again, he said, 'When you came here before, the Soviet Union was a strong country, feared abroad and safe at home. Now Moscow is a third-rate Las Vegas with crime and disorder rampant: the centre of a country which is weak and a laughing stock to the world. Which do you prefer?'

On that first visit to Russia we held a formal meeting with the relevant minister in his large office in the Kremlin accompanied by an interpreter who was dressed in Carnaby Street modern. I made my little speech, addressing him as Excellency in every paragraph: 'We are so interested to try and bring some of the popular culture that we have in music in England and in return we are so pleased that occasionally we do get some Russian music played in London. We are anxious, Excellency, to know whether we would be welcome, and whether it would be possible for the Rolling Stones to perform here. Four years ago you may know that there was rather an unfortunate political event in Altamont, California, when the police got very nervous and there was actually a death, but that was exceptional and that was the American police keeping order.'

The minister then answered, 'I am afraid, my dear Prince, that you have misunderstood the aims of Russian culture. We are not prepared to have these vandals and cultural nobodies teaching the reprehensible lessons which they practise in Western Europe. All that I can say to you is if you come over you should be aware that should any Russian citizens involved in any concerts be caught with drugs, they will be open to the utmost rigours of our Soviet law. And for those who have come from England or other parts of the Western world, we will simply have a plane in permanent readiness for you at four o'clock in the morning or whenever we notice these things and you will be firmly but kindly expelled.

'I should also point out to you that you may have noticed that we have a friendly arrangement whereby there is a concierge on every floor of our hotels. One of her jobs is to see that women who are not married do not enter the rooms of unaccompanied men at night-time. Do I make myself perfectly clear? Now I hope that you will be happy to take some tickets at the Bolshoi which we have got for you for tomorrow night to mark our pleasure of thanking you for your visit.'

It was indeed all quite clear. George St George said, 'I told you it was probably a wild-goose chase, but at least you have been here and met the minister.' We went to the Bolshoi Theatre, where we were ushered into the former royal box and given champagne with the programmes; I saw photographers peeping out from behind curtains and taking pictures of us. Back in London I reported the conversation to the Stones, who said, 'Thank goodness you were able to find out before we went. We may have to wait a few more years', which we did – more than fifteen years in the end.

In contrast, on the large tours of the States, New Orleans was always comfortable, welcoming and fascinating because of its history – in turn part of Spanish, French, and then British America – and the jazz that had originated around

Bourbon Street. One very much felt that the city was different from the rest of mainland America and even from the rest of the Louisiana Purchase. The Garden District, which had been fashionable at the turn of the century, was a slum.

We had the greatest fun imaginable. My friend Marguerite Littmann, Louisiana-born and bred, was one of the pivots around which the city's society revolved – her friends were the old world of New Orleans. Her brother was the novelist and playwright Speed Lamkin, who in the early 1950s had achieved some success with his first novel, *Tiger in the Garden*, describing the old 'plantation set'.

Marguerite had been, it was said, the inspiration for Holly Golightly in Truman Capote's *Breakfast at Tiffany's*. I already knew Truman quite well through my New York friends C. Z. Guest and Mrs Paley: he used to stay in St Moritz at the same time as all of us were there and, indeed, came to London as well. He asked me early on whether the Stones would like it if he came and wrote a piece about them. I asked the band and they were very happy for him to do so.

He took along Jackie Onassis's sister Lee Radziwill – who had been at the White Ball – and spent time with the Stones. In the end, alas, he did not produce the article, which *Rolling Stone* magazine were hoping to publish. It was a disappointment for me, as I was hoping that Truman would answer the question which to me was the key question of an intelligent observer: what was it that constituted the Rolling Stones' great success and popularity? The magazine dispatched Andy Warhol to interview Capote about his impressions. He commented on Mick's 'remarkable quality of being absolutely able to be totally extroverted', noting as I had that Mick's skill lay not in his singing ability but in his showmanship.

Marguerite introduced us to Tennessee Williams. She had taught Elizabeth Taylor, she said, to talk 'Southern' for *A Streetcar Named Desire* (the *New York Times* once wrote that Marguerite herself had 'a voice you could marinade ham in'). Williams possessed enormous charm; one could see what a great man he was. Unfortunately he was also a very close friend of Jack Daniel's and one had to be rather lucky, which we were periodically, in having good conversations with him.

We would organise parties for our friends who had travelled down from New York. Mick and Keith loved the local musicians who came and played. At one hotel, the owner, Jimmy Coleman, flew in daily deliveries of oysters from Brittany. Marguerite pointed out that it was a mark of great distinction when a family had somebody who had jumped off one of the bridges in New Orleans and committed suicide, and apparently one of the Coleman clan had duly obliged.

On one tour, Marguerite arranged for her friend Matilda Stream, one of the great ladies of New Orleans, who owned probably the best collection of Fabergé outside the English royal family, to organise a party for the Stones at her delightful old-fashioned plantation house on the banks of the Mississippi, where we had lunch, looking over the slave quarters and imagining how it must have been *ante bellum*.

At the luncheon, which was on a day when there was going to be a Stones show in the evening, Matilda took me aside and said, 'Since this seems to be quite an occasion, I've decided that I will come to the concert and my son Spook shall take me there.' I had not thought to offer her any tickets because I could not imagine she would have wanted to go. I said, 'Of course', and we gave her VIP tickets and placed her in boxes where we had all our friends. A young man who worked for me in my office in London, Alexander Ogilvie-Grant, had the job of looking after our friends, seeing that they were happy and making sure that they all left before the last song, to avoid the mad crush on the way out. Alexander asked me, 'Surely they'd want to see the end of the show?' 'No, no,' I said, 'it's far more important for these people to get away *before* the crowd leaves.'

Half an hour after the Stones had started their performance I was wandering around backstage and noticed Matilda and her son Spook walking away. I caught up with them. 'Matilda, are you enjoying yourself?' 'No,' she said, 'I am not. They are five ugly, and pointless young men, and I *loathe* their music.' So I said, 'In that case, perhaps you are right to leave.' Compared to the usual star-struck response, I thought Matilda's was a refreshing, if unusual, attitude.

The often insurmountable gulf between the classical music world and the rock industry was made all too clear to me by Yehudi Menuhin. During one of the first Stones tours I was involved in, probably the first tour where I had managed to see to it that the band made some significant money from touring – which in the past, of course, they never had – there was a major concert coming up at Earls Court, which had some magnificent and startling décor, and a vast flower that opened up on the stage out of which the Stones appeared.

I had recently initiated a course of action, something that the Stones did from then on, where the band would give a significant sum of their profits to charity (which we always matched). When we were talking about potential recipients in England, I had suggested that an appropriate one might be the Yehudi Menuhin School in Surrey, and that we could perhaps set up a Rolling Stones Scholarship for some of the students there. The Stones were delighted with the idea.

I placed a call to Menuhin, and once I had had a discussion with one of his staff about the tickets to Earls Court that we were proposing to give the school as part of the arrangement, I asked Yehudi, 'Will you want to come to the concert?' He said, 'The awful thing is that I don't think I can come on that day, because the night before I am playing in Stuttgart and I may be obliged to play there twice, once in the evening, so I'm afraid I'm not going to be able to take up your offer. Though of course my music school will be very grateful for the Rolling Stones' generosity.'

On the day of the concert I received a desperate call from Menuhin's assistant, saying, 'Sir Yehudi has just telephoned to say that he is not playing the second concert in Stuttgart tonight, so he would *love* to come, and he will be there.' I suggested that, given the shortness of time, as soon as Menuhin arrived in London he should come straight over to our house and have some dinner with us before going on to Earls Court, which was nearby.

Menuhin arrived terribly late, the poor man; his train connections had been delayed. He was rather lingering over dinner so I said, 'I really think we should get going, because the Stones will be coming onstage very shortly, and that's what's exciting for you to see.' I was getting constant calls from the venue, saying 'It really does look as if the band will be on in quarter of an hour', and a great panic set in. We rushed over to Earls Court, went at some pace through the backstage area, and just in time reached our seats next to the mixer. The show started almost immediately.

After no more than ten minutes, Menuhin turned to me and shouted above the music, 'I can't take this any more. I'm afraid I have to leave. So would you come with me?' Josephine and I, unbelievably embarrassed, got up with him, as did a couple of the friends who had been at dinner with us, and back we trooped through the backstage area, where all of the Stones' wives, girlfriends and friends were, all longing to speak to the great violinist. But he didn't wait to stop and chat with them; we got straight into the car and were driven back to Holland Villas Road.

As we drew up, I saw that the road was blocked by some vast television trucks drawn up outside our front door. 'Ah, I thought they'd be here by now,' Menuhin said. 'What do you mean?' I asked. 'Well, you see, I said that I would give them an interview after I had heard the Stones. I knew you wouldn't mind.'

I was livid. But what could I do? Menuhin parked himself in my drawing room with half a dozen camera people and a pack of journalists. Luckily we had a library on the first floor, so Josephine and I were able to take our other guests up there, where we entertained ourselves for an hour or so while the interviews continued. There was a knock at the door. It was Menuhin, popping his head round to say, 'Thank you so much, so kind of you. Now I must go because I have to leave for Brussels first thing tomorrow.'

When I picked up my copy of *The Times* the next morning, I found a ghastly interview with Menuhin from the night before, describing the Stones' show. The gist of it was, 'Meaningless cacophony. Overgrown children pandering to the worst emotions one can have, playing what they thought was music, and all I could think of was some barbaric ritual. Awful.'

We were giving a big party at Annabel's, Mark Birley's club, to celebrate the end of the tour. Keith was clearly the most upset about the article. 'Surely he could have seen something in our music,' he said. 'Yes,' I said. 'All he had to do was to read the score. It would not have been difficult for him to do that.' I had, incidentally, suggested that to Menuhin, and he had assured me he did have the sheet music of the Stones' songs, but if he did clearly he had not looked at it.

I wrote a letter to him saying that naturally I was not commenting on whether he liked the music or not, but on his lack of manners in taking their money and not, as it were, drinking a toast to the hard work and professional performance he had witnessed.

Not long afterwards Josephine went to a dinner party given by Malcolm Sargent where the Menuhins were invited. Josephine said to Yehudi's wife Diana, 'This thing about your husband being a man of deep goodness, how could he have justified not giving a generous interview by saying something more like, "It's not my kind of music but hats off to a great performance"? That would have been easy to do.' 'Oh well,' said Diana Menuhin, 'I'm sure he didn't really *mean* what he said.'

Our friend Princess Peg of Hesse, née Geddes – she had gone on holiday to Bavaria in the 1930s, where she met the German Prince Ludwig of Hesse-Darmstadt and married him shortly before the war – gave wonderful concerts at her house at Wolfsgarten, south of Frankfurt. She was a dedicated patron of the arts, especially music, and was a great supporter of Benjamin Britten and Peter Pears' Aldeburgh Festival.

'What is Menuhin like when he stays with you?' I asked her. 'He's a split character,' she told me. 'In one way he is absolutely marvellous: excellent company, very intuitive, very pleasant. But suddenly he can change so quickly you don't know what's hitting you. He can be extraordinarily disagreeable. It's very odd. But I don't care. I like him, he likes me, and we have our wonderful concerts. But I'm not surprised by your story.'

After a show in Frankfurt, Mick was once taken by our friend Prince Rupert Hohenlohe, whose sister was an assistant of Princess Peg, to the Princess's house, where she asked Mick to engrave his name with a diamond on the famous window she had there, the window panes covered with amazing signatures from writers, musicians, politicians and the crowned heads of Europe.

Mick was, I am sure, not that bothered by Yehudi Menuhin's comments. Although I know he enjoys seventeenth-century Italian music – Corelli, Scarlatti – on CD, I am not sure that classical music plays a huge part in his life. Shortly after Mick and I had got to know each other, the great pianist Vladimir Horowitz was playing in London, for the first time in many years. I said to Mick, 'I've got some tickets. Do you want to come, because you'll never have heard somebody of that age and that quality in the flesh.' He didn't want to, and came up with a series of excuses as to why.

I am sure Keith would have leapt at the chance to go to the concert. When I had first been in Keith and Anita's house in the South of France while they were recording *Exile On Main Street*, I noticed that, although they had barely unpacked – there were boxes and crates everywhere – he did have a pile of LPs out. And the ones that caught my eye were Bach's *48 Preludes and Fugues*. He had taken the trouble to bring them out in the luggage from England.

7

'Corruption never has been compulsory'

Anthony Eden

All the time that I worked with the Stones I never changed my habits, my clothes or my attitudes. I did not pretend to be overwhelmed by or to enter into discussions about their music.

I was never tempted by the rock'n'roll lifestyle. Although I enjoyed a good vintage wine, I was never a heavy drinker, nor a drug-taker. I always aimed to maintain a strict discipline backstage, for security reasons, and tried to see that the band and the entourage did not get drunk or disorderly. I felt, and still feel, that remaining true to myself stood us in good stead whenever problems arose.

The Stones had their own dressing rooms or their own caravans where, in the privacy of their own space, Keith, Mick and the other artists could do whatever they wanted. What went on behind those closed doors was entirely their business. I understood that it was part of their own particular way of preparing for a show.

I went to see them backstage only if I needed to talk to them about some specific or current problem; if they needed to sign a document, perhaps, or if I had to bring somebody important along for them to see. I'd say to them, 'I have the head of EMI Publishing coming to the show. He wants to meet you and I would very much like you to see him.' They would then emerge from their respective lairs, becoming friendly hosts to these outsiders.

We very soon formalised this policy of the 'meet and greet'. At a specific time, just before they went onstage, the Stones would be on hand to meet – and greet – some of the people who were important for their career. It was quite often the only time that these businessmen would ever have the opportunity to come into direct, personal contact with the band. They could go back and tell their colleagues and their wives and girlfriends that they had met Mick Jagger. The Stones for their part would be on their very best behaviour. They knew that at a show not only did they have to give a superb performance but they also had to look like intelligent, with-it business people.

One of the aspects of touring that I had to bring to the band's attention was the cost of the exercise. On the early tours I was particularly struck by how extremely professional the Stones were onstage and how quickly they were able to radiate that elusive star quality. The atmosphere was very good. Of course, achieving that atmosphere came with a price tag attached.

Whenever I held business meetings with the band I would invite the relevant lawyer and accountant to attend so that any figures or contractual points could be gone through there and then. I was always very careful to make my estimates quite conservative, and I would point out to the band facts about the costs, about which they had not the faintest idea.

Before a tour, I would need to be quite clear: 'This is what it will cost to mount this production, which means you will have to have at least twenty gigs making x amount of profit to clear off the production costs before you see one single penny.' I tried to encourage them to reduce the expenses in certain ways, for example not letting the entire tour personnel stay in the grandest hotel in town.

Having all the people they employed or whom they simply liked travelling with on the tour and staying in five-star hotels was madness. The tour party would already be paid a per diem, the daily amount for living expenses. On top of that, at a five-star hotel getting one shirt laundered might cost ten dollars instead of fifty cents at the local laundrette, and an orange juice or gin and tonic five times the normal price. Saving those expenses could make a huge difference. 'You do realise who's paying for them,' I would reiterate. '*You* are paying for them, and you have no need to do so.'

One day, quite out of the blue, I was contacted by the manager of a theatre company which included actors of the stature of Laurence Olivier and John Gielgud. He said, 'You'll think this rather strange, but I have been told by somebody I know that you run these tours for the Rolling Stones. Would you be prepared to run a tour for *us*?'

I said I would love to do that, and asked him a couple of questions: 'What sort of hotels do you stay at?' 'Oh, the cheapest you can find. And we make people double up in the rooms.' I said, 'You mean Gielgud and Olivier are prepared to double up?' 'Yes, that's all right, they'll muck in.' 'And what about per diems?' 'Per diems, what are they?' 'They are the daily expenses we pay the tour entourage so that they can get something to eat and drink.''Well, all that the actors need is a sandwich and a half pint of beer.' I was highly amused by that and relayed the conversation to the Stones with great gusto.

I also tried to make sense of the hierarchy within the touring party. In the past, all the personnel who were working on the tour would be able to come into the tour room, have some drinks, relax by playing pool, all using one badge. There was another badge to get into the caravan or the dressing rooms of the artist. Over the years we refined this to something approaching an art form.

I made a note in a journal I kept during a later tour: 'One guest on tour was amazed by the efficiency and hierarchy of the organisation. Just like a court: rivals, whispering, grades of status granting access with others being used to fetch and carry. Others do everything for one including guard, protect, transport, feed and flatter ... and perhaps poison as well.'

As well as attempting to reduce the unnecessary costs, I also turned my attention to improving the income from touring. I saw that tours could be converted into moneymaking operations as opposed to the band simply 'working the album' for the benefit of the record company. Working the album meant that the band were told they were touring as part of a promotion to raise the profile of their latest album and increase sales, because the money was going to come from the sale of records. As far as the tour was concerned the record company would pay a very modest sum as 'tour expenses'.

In the early days the Stones had undertaken a number of tours, the first few organised by Andrew Oldham, the later tours under the control of Allen Klein after he had come on board. The remarkable thing about those tours was that, although people loved going to the shows and the band gained an enormous amount of publicity and goodwill from touring – and the girls screaming and shouting were undoubtedly highly ego-enhancing for the band – no money ever came into their pockets.

In 1969, shortly after I had first met Mick, the Stones were keen to do a new tour but they did not want it to be in Klein's hands. Mick discussed this with me, and I told him, 'As you well know I have not done any tours before, but let me think about this and see how it could work.'

The person who wanted to organise the tour was a nephew of Allen Klein's, Ronald Schneider. I met Ronald a few times and came away thinking that he at least had the advantage of being Klein's nephew, he knew the American market and understood both rock'n'roll and the Stones. Of course he had the distinct *dis*advantage of being Klein's nephew as well . . . However, given the circumstances, Mick and I decided that we would allow him to run the tour but that I would control the money. I felt it was vital that we used high-quality auditors, and so we went to Arthur Anderson, who were Leopold Joseph's auditors. Ronald Schneider was living in Miami at the time; Arthur Anderson's office in London informed me that the company had a branch in Miami and that they were sure the branch could handle matters perfectly efficiently.

The tour took place and went extremely well, with all the tickets being sold out, but at the very end, in December 1969, there was the Altamont free concert, where violence between members of the crowd and the Hell's Angels who were ostensibly in charge of security led to the death of eighteen-year-old Meredith Hunter. The band knew the mood offstage was menacing, but were unaware that this young man had been stabbed and killed.

A couple of days after the Altamont concert I had been scheduled to meet Mick in Geneva to work out the band's foreign bank accounts as part of all the financial arrangements we were gradually putting in place for them. When I heard what had happened in California, I contacted Mick's secretary, Jo Bergman, whom I liked very much and trusted, to ask if Mick was still coming. 'Oh yes,' she said, 'he'll be arriving on this flight, and I'll be with him.' Of course, the papers interpreted this by saying that Mick had fled California for Switzerland... When Mick arrived there were two main topics for discussion: the financial arrangements and the appalling killing at Altamont.

Mick said, 'We will have to have a serious think about what this means for us.' I replied that I thought that in so far as there was any publicity it would demonstrate the gigantic operation that the tour was, how strong Mick and the band's performances had been and that, apart from that one tragic and untimely incident, the people who had gone to the shows had been happy. We both spoke to people that we knew, and the idea came to Mick and myself that releasing a film of the tour would be fascinating since it would show the truth of the matter. That, of course, was the Maysles brothers' film *Gimme Shelter*, which was excellent – the best tour film the Stones ever made, I think, not least because it had a serious point to make. It showed that there was concern about these huge gatherings, and, given the death of this young man, that there had to be some form of order and proper security brought to bear on similar events.

I spoke to an American friend of mine, whom I had known

socially before, and who had an association with the cinema side of Warners. 'I've got to ask you something very odd. I want you to look me in the eye, and tell me that you will make sure, because of our old friendship, that the interests of the Rolling Stones will be looked after since I do not yet have the experience of the true costs of film production.' He replied, 'That is an amazing request to the other side in a deal, but I do see what you mean.' So during the course of the film production I at least knew that I had an ally within the film company.

Arthur Anderson produced their report. There was very little money because we had to stump up some funding for the film production before it happened and although Albert and David Maysles were very talented, they had nothing to contribute financially. I had a terrible battle trying to get our side credited and paid the infinitesimal amount of money that there was, but it worked out and the film had a great *succès d'estime*, and in fact focused my mind on thinking that touring was clearly an area where the band could make money.

By 1972, locked in the interminable legal wrangling with Allen Klein, it was no longer appropriate to have his nephew Ronald involved, even though he had been a success on that previous tour. I asked Mick and Keith (it was Keith who had picked Ronnie Schneider) if they could now think of anyone else they would like to have as a tour director. Amongst other names they suggested Peter Rudge, who had already fulfilled that role for The Who, and whom they knew and liked. Peter, it transpired, was interested in expanding his activities away from working solely for The Who, and took up our offer.

While Peter Rudge was directing his first tour, the Hell's Angels wanted to handle all the security. Peter later regaled us all with long stories about the Hell's Angels crowding in on him in a hotel in New York, taking him and dangling him bodily out of a window on the fiftieth floor to make sure he took their advice. Fact or fiction, the stories did put us on our guard and reminded us all that we had to be incredibly careful not to do anything foolish. There were two main areas where one would expect foolishness to occur: being caught taking drugs and being found taking cash without a contract, thereby trying to avoid taxes, especially as we had to remember that tax rates both in the States and England were still vertiginously high.

Previously, unaccounted cash delivered to the band and their management in a paper bag had been the norm. Any cash business is a fertile breeding ground for crime and corruption, of course. Bands were only too delighted to receive parcels of money but failed to realise they were thereby participating in a huge tax fraud. That was something I was rigorously determined to see changed.

Slowly but surely we were able to alter how tours operated, but even on the tour which took place in 1978 at the time of *Some Girls*, an album which generated exceptionally good record sales and very strong ticket sales at the major venues in Los Angeles and New York, somebody, an accountant or one of the tour personnel, came up and asked me, 'What do we do with the $50,000 in this paper bag?' I said, 'You give it straight to the auditors.'

I summoned the Stones and told them, 'This is the most dangerous thing that you have had to deal with, apart from the drugs busts in London. A tax fraud in the United States could really halt your career, so I am afraid the paper bag of dollar bills will have to go back into your taxable income. But there we are.' We could not be party to receiving undeclared income.

Scalping tickets – the reselling of concert tickets – was another area of great concern. I had noticed that tickets were being scalped, but everyone I spoke to about it said, 'There's nothing you can do about that. That's the promoter's business. Do you want the Stones' children to be kidnapped? You should be aware that you are dealing with difficult and potentially dangerous people.'

One of the worst examples of scalping came when we worked with Bill Graham, the West Coast promoter who had made his name with the Fillmore West and Winterland in San Francisco during the late sixties, at the height of the Summer of Love. Graham, in my eyes, was an old-fashioned mythomaniac. He would tell bands, 'If you want to be popular and have a lasting career in this business, you need to give the people the chance of getting cheap tickets', which, of course, went down very well with the Stones, thinking that they were helping the less well off listen to their music and come to see the act. Promoters behaved in a very crude way by playing up to bands' wishes to give young people who had no money access to their music.

What Bill Graham always omitted to tell the Stones – but which I realised early on – was that the cheaper the face value of the ticket the more money could and would disappear into the pockets of various associates of the promoter when the tickets were subsequently scalped for up to $100 or more.

On a nightly basis we would be checking with our auditors that we had accounting for all the tickets sold and delivered. But that did not and could not show the level of scalping. If a ticket was scalped at $50, $10 or $15 of that amount would have gone to the local promoter, and a tour director might take the same amount to bring the 'amount received' down to the face value of the ticket.

Scalping was endemic, all-pervasive. Touring, at the time, was essentially a deeply corrupt business. At one point, out of the five main promoters in Germany, three had received jail sentences and two were under investigation.

Record companies were equally complicit in the scalping: they needed tickets to bribe the disc jockeys to give singles airtime and record stores to stock the releases, and were constantly trying to persuade us to provide free tickets, which they would then sell on and pocket the cash. I remember a conversation with one executive at CBS when the Stones were on that label.

The executive complained, 'This is ridiculous. We are buying your records. Don't you understand that we've got to spread a few tickets around?' I said, 'Yes, but if reading is also one of the gifts that you gained from your education, then in your contract you will see that you can get the amount of tickets you want, and at the designated price.' He got highly agitated about the fact that we didn't give them as many tickets as they thought they should receive. But I did enjoy that conversation.

A variation on the scalping theme was that friends of Bill Graham's in San Francisco were given different tickets and told to enter the theatre through a certain turnstile which had been tampered with so that it did not register anybody passing through. The money for those tickets was never accounted for. The information about this came from people lower down in the Bill Graham organisation, who discussed it with their peers in the Stones' organisation and it was reported to me.

We therefore had a major flare-up with Graham, which required recomputing all the monies, but, surprisingly, when it came to the lawsuit that I was going to bring, not one of the people who had given us verbal evidence about these activities would provide an affidavit, from which one could only draw the conclusion that they had been 'talked to', and were scared stiff of bringing down on themselves the ire of the people concerned.

As a result of the changes we put in place, it did become more difficult for promoters to continue these scams, which was not so easy for many of the groups whose management was directly involved with accumulating profit from these practices.

I sought advice from people who were in the music business. The father of Steve Rubell, who ran Studio 54 in New York, was a leading New York promoter. (In passing, I remember one evening at Studio 54 when Josephine danced with Mikhail Baryshnikov, which, oddly enough, she herself does not remember.)

So I asked Steve, 'What can one do about this?' He told me, 'You'll never be able to get rid of it entirely, there'll always be a skim. What you have to do is see that it is no more than that. You need to negotiate with the promoters so that they are aware that you are aware what's happening. It is impossible to have a policeman standing next to every turnstile, but nonetheless you will know what's going on.' And that was very important.

I had to come to terms with the fact that there was an irreducible core of approximately 10 per cent that would never come our way, and that we should concentrate on securing and accounting for all of the remaining 90 per cent. What that meant in reality was that if somebody was the promoter for a venue like Shea Stadium, where the audience could be 100,000 people, the number of seats not sold would not impact too much on the overall sale. I certainly didn't like it, but I had to learn to accept some of the realities of the music business. I could not change everything single-handed.

Dealing with the touring industry people required a certain amount of adjustment in my business philosophy. Not everybody, for example, was prepared to sign a contract. I was once entering into an agreement with Howard Kaufman, who managed the band Chicago amongst other acts, a very, very shrewd customer. He told me, 'Rupert, I am not going to sign a contract. I'm going to do this job, I won't take more than what you've said, but I won't sign a contract. I am not prepared to enter into any form of legal discussion on what I do and what I don't do. You'll have to take that as a risk.'

When I reported this back to Mick, I said, 'Oddly enough, I think it is worth doing, because I have never heard anybody else be quite as honest about this.' However, when that particular tour reached Los Angeles, I received information about a high level of scalping going on. I had a meeting with Howard Kaufman and asked him what the hell was happening. 'Well, I did buy quite a lot of tickets, in various places. And that's what I did. I put up my money, I bought my tickets, and if I'm selling them or not selling them, that is my business ...'

Merchandising sales and car parking charges were routinely siphoned off and undeclared. The merchandising was the same as the scalping, only worse, because it was so much more blatant. There was always somebody handling the merchandising who apparently only produced modest sums of money, some significantly more modest than others.

Much later, in the 1990s, when the Canadian promoter Michael Cohl was running the tours for the Stones, he was looking round a particular venue in Italy and could not see any official merchandising stands, even though on his way in he had passed by plenty of unofficial stands selling merchandise that was clearly completely different in shape, size and quality from the products Michael was selling for the tour.

He was naturally very annoyed and asked to speak to the local promoter. Eventually the promoter turned up accompanied by a *carabiniere*, who said, 'Come this way.' They all went into the promoter's office, where the *carabiniere* took his gun out, placed it on the table, and said to Michael, 'You will not change the merchandising arrangements. Goodbye.' That was corruption at its most brutal and unsubtle.

One of the key elements in the Rolling Stones merchandising was the tongue logo. The tongue was the most successful side product of setting up the Rolling Stones record label, because it gave the Stones a globally recognisable brand. Mick had found the illustrator, John Pasche, and I thought the logo was excellent. Later on, when we started making significant amounts of money out of merchandising, the illegal copying became an issue: the level of bootlegging was gigantic.

I eventually became very concerned about the illegal use of the logo and covered the copyright in a batch of countries, an incredibly expensive undertaking. At one stage we were paying more than a million dollars a year for copyright protection, and we only made any real money during the periods when the band were on tour.

Rolling Stones Records had been established under the direction of Earl McGrath, a great friend of both Ahmet Ertegun and me. The proposition was that a label fronted by the Stones might be attractive to groups and their managers and that albums could be distributed through Atlantic to make some additional money for the band. This was a phase when major bands felt that having their own label was a way to expand their activities. The Beatles, of course, had Apple; Led Zeppelin started Swan Song Records; and Emerson, Lake & Palmer launched Manticore.

Although the Rolling Stones label had a minor success with *Bush Doctor*, an album by Peter Tosh from Bob Marley's band The Wailers, projects by other artists, including John Phillips of the Mamas & the Papas and the Cuban band Kracker, either failed to sell well or failed to be released (the John Phillips album was never completed, but along the way cost Atlantic a huge amount of money). In the end the Rolling Stones Records label served primarily as an outlet for solo projects by the group, and their own albums appeared under the logo.

Earl McGrath's wife came from a well-known Italian family called Pecci-Blunt. Josephine and I both knew her, and her brother Dino had been my boss at Bache in Rome in the early 1960s. When Earl got the job as the manager of Rolling Stones Records, he proved to be very good at handling the record cover artwork, because he was a picture dealer. Earl's great strength was that he was as close to Keith as he was to Mick and so he was very important in liaising between them.

The concern of bands for their fanbase could obscure them from the commercial realities. That was typified by groups' obsession with cover design, which was certainly true of the Stones. When they were discussing the artwork, which Earl used to do with Mick in the first instance, there were always terrible problems over whether it should be purple or yellow, a poodle rather than a dachshund, three girls rather than five, two black girls rather than one – it went on and on and on.

I remember hearing a story about the moment when Peter

Grant, the manager of Led Zeppelin, delivered an album to Ahmet Ertegun. Ahmet was very fond of and amused by Peter Grant, but he, Peter, was fastidious – just like Mick – about album covers. Peter Grant had the album delivered, and came round the next day to the Atlantic offices to ask Ahmet what he thought of it. Ahmet kept him waiting, then said, 'I don't know what to say to you. But I'm not having it in blue. The colour's got to be green', or whichever colour it was. Peter Grant was most disturbed. 'But that surely doesn't matter so much, it's the music you're after.' Despite the considerable force of his personality, Peter lost the argument, but gained the colour.

Alongside merchandising was the whole issue of sponsorship. At concert venues we would see huge sponsorship banners, but no money coming into us. One time in France, before a show in Nice, I asked Bill Graham about these banners. 'Oh,' he replied, 'that's all handled by the local promoters.' I said, 'No, that has to change. We will negotiate with the major industrial companies, and you will have to help them put up the advertising.' He was furious.

There was no backstage lounge at the venue so he had to take me down to the gents' lavatories, shouting at me, 'This is absolutely impossible, you're ruining my career.' I simply said, 'This is the way it is going. That is the end of the discussion. Now, is there anything else you want to do down here?'

There is a story, possibly apocryphal, about the early days of Coca-Cola in Atlanta, Georgia, some time during the First World War. The head of the company was sitting in his office. His secretary, very embarrassed, told him that a young gentleman was desperate to see the chairman and they had not been able to persuade him to go away. 'All right,' said the chairman, 'we'll send Jim to talk to him.' Jim was the number two in the company.

So off Jim went to talk to him. 'No, I'm talking only to the boss,' insisted the young man. 'And I will want the chairman to sign this piece of paper, saying that in return for my idea Coca-Cola will use it and pay me one million dollars if they make more than that.' Eventually they relented and he was ushered into the chairman's office. He persuaded the chairman to sign the piece of paper. 'Now, young man, what is your great story?' And he heard two words in response: 'Bottle it.' At the time the Coca-Cola company were only selling the drink through soda fountains. 'Bottle it.' And, sure enough, it was only once the company started selling Coca-Cola in the iconic glass bottle in 1916 that the brand really took off.

General Electric was, I think, the first company to sponsor a tour. The people there were delighted with the concept and had never thought of it – the rock'n'roll equivalent of the 'Bottle it' story. The band, however, were not happy: 'General Electric?' They were suspicious of any corporate organisation. I said, 'What do you care? You are not doing anything dishonest but selling a business product.'

By 1978, most of my time was spent working on Rolling Stones business, and that coincided with Mick taking me aside and saying he would like me to be on tour for longer periods of time than I had been before. I said, 'Would a third of the dates be enough?' He said, 'I hope so.' From that point on I always had a room booked wherever they played, whereas previously I had gone only for a few days and to sort out something specific.

Shortly before that exchange, there was one very significant and potentially career-shattering moment in the life of the

Stones. The contract with Atlantic had come up for renegotia-
tion. I had turned down Atlantic because they counter-offered
a deal which was not as attractive as I wanted. I was leaning
towards recommending that the Stones signed with the
Philips/Siemens company Polygram.

I was in Los Angeles in February 1977, staying at the Beverly
Hills Hotel. When I arrived in my room there was a magnum
of Krug from Ahmet Ertegun at Atlantic, some Bollinger
from MCA and a bottle of dubious American champagne
from Robert Stigwood at RSO. As I rang to thank everybody,
I heard Ahmet hooting with laughter down the phone saying,
'You do realise the cheap champagne didn't really come from
Stigwood. *I* sent that!'

A day or two later I was ready to enter the final stages of
negotiation with the various parties involved, when I took a
telephone call from Mick, who said he had to warn me that
Keith had just been arrested in Canada for peddling, but not
using, heroin. It was all going to come out in the press the next
day and he thought I would need to know that, especially
given the state of play on the contracts.

I had to ring up in turn all of the people with whom I had
been negotiating and tell them the news. 'This has come out
and I just wanted to make sure that you are still in for what
you said.' One by one each record company dropped out.
Only Ahmet Ertegun stayed loyal in the face of such a
serious blow. In due course I went back to Ahmet Ertegun
and said that he and I should both concede all the small
contractual points that we had been arguing about. And
Ahmet said, 'Of course.'

As the legal case against Keith continued, the future of the
band was under an immense cloud – the prospect of the Stones

playing without him was, to most people, and most of all to Keith, inconceivable.

As soon as Mick had called me I had immediately started working behind the scenes to get a good lawyer to help us. I had also had to build into the contractual discussions that we would have to change the basis by which 'the Rolling Stones' were defined. We would commit to produce 'Mick Jagger and two of the Rolling Stones'.

When I went through the wording of the contract I showed Keith the paragraph in the letter in which I had set that out. 'Keith,' I said, 'I am afraid the sting is in the tail of this letter.' He was understandably most concerned. But to give him credit for his professionalism, he did not make a scene about it. He understood why it had to be worded in that way, although he was distraught that this had happened.

My contacts in Canada and Washington both said that the likelihood was that Keith would receive a prison sentence, even if only suspended. I am sure that Keith also thought that he would be going to prison. In the end we avoided that although he was banned for coming in for work during a certain period of time, which we managed to overcome through a specialised lawyer who had good contacts within the immigration authorities.

In the legal presentations we had concentrated on the fact that (and I remember the phrase that I thought of) rich people tend to buy ten packets of Cornflakes for their kitchen cupboard in one go, and could then buy more as was needed, but you would never say that they were dealing in Cornflakes. This was the same thing: a rich man had bought a lot of heroin for his personal use because he thought the price was good. The argument may have helped, but it was a very dicey moment.

The suggestion was made that Keith should play a benefit concert; the judge and our lawyers agreed to this as part of the negotiations. The concert was to raise money for the Canadian Institute of the Blind. Keith remarked, 'Why not a concert for the deaf . . . ?'

We always had to be very careful every time we crossed a frontier. In certain countries, like Japan, being caught with drugs would mean instant prison, so we could not be even the slightest bit relaxed. We had to speak to all the security people, and the heads of every department in the tour party and stress time and again, 'For God's sake, see that there are no drugs in anybody's luggage.'

My view was that if somebody wanted to take too much alcohol and too many drugs once they were an adult, that was their choice and their life, but what I was most concerned about was the illegality and the possibility of a drugs arrest stopping a tour.

8

'They always say time changes things, but you
actually have to change them yourself'

Andy Warhol

The incident with Keith and the drugs charges in Canada
seemed to mark – or perhaps underscore – a perceptible shift
in the dynamics within the band. There was certainly a sense
of change in the air.

Keith's bust, and the prospect of a spell in prison, was
undoubtedly a factor in his own growing up. When I had first
seen him after the news broke, it was not in any way an uncomfortable meeting, because he knew that I was going to be
involved in trying to work things out for him, to resolve a very
awkward situation. He was not particularly apologetic about
what had happened – if at all – not that I was expecting or
asking him to be. That was his business. But he had a very
human attitude to what might occur: he was going to have to
get used to the fact that he was no longer a riotous youth but
a serious adult. Certainly the very real threat to his ability to
make music as part of the Rolling Stones would have sobered
him up. Music was always, and still is, his first mistress.

At this time Keith's relationship with Anita Pallenberg was nearing its end. I had known Anita from the first days that I started working with the band. She was the descendant of the Swiss symbolist painter Arnold Böcklin on the paternal side of the family (her father, Arnaldo, was also an artist), and through her German mother, Paula Wiederhold, she was descended from one of the great German actors. Indeed, when I met her she looked set for a significant film career, having already appeared in Roger Vadim's *Barbarella*, and in Donald Cammell and Nick Roeg's *Performance* alongside Mick.

But she was gravely obsessed with heroin – to such a degree that even Keith could not take it. At least, that is what I thought. It is, of course, remarkable that they both survived those years. Shortly after the Toronto bust and its aftermath, Keith and Anita had gone through a further drama, when a teenage boy shot himself in the head at the house that she and Keith shared in upstate New York; Keith was recording in a studio in Paris at the time. The press was full of wild rumours. These were clearly troubled times for them and effectively marked the end of their life as a couple.

Keith then formed a relationship with the model Patti Hansen, a beautiful girl, eventually marrying her in 1983, on his fortieth birthday, with Mick as best man. Patti had grown up in Staten Island and came from Norwegian stock, a family of respectable God-fearing, Bible-reading Scandinavians. She brought, I felt, some much needed stability into Keith's life.

Mick was also going through a major change in his own life.

He and Bianca were getting divorced after seven years of marriage. They had got married in May 1971 in the town hall at St Tropez during the recording sessions for *Exile On Main Street*, although I had not attended the wedding. This was a strategic decision since I had worked for Mick on what in French is called the *séparation des biens*, whereby both parties keep their own assets in the event of divorce. I thought it better that I should not even be present at the wedding. I did not wish to compromise myself if I ever had to be involved in the drafting of such documents. I stayed away. Josephine, however, did go, riding in a convertible with Stephen Stills to head into the media scrum that surrounded the ceremony and the reception.

Thus it was that, following their separation, when I sat down with Bianca to arrange their settlement I said to her – as indeed I would to Jerry Hall two decades later – 'I have to make it clear to you that as far as this business is concerned I am Mick's man. I am not your man, and therefore you must speak to your own lawyer about anything that I suggest to you because I am trying to do the best that I can for Mick.' It was fairest on both parties, I thought, to be totally frank and open about this from the outset.

'However,' I said, 'I do have a proposal for you here which is that you should ask a close friend of yours whom you trust to discuss these matters with me, because it is possible that we could resolve this whole problem first, only going to lawyers when the financial terms have been worked out. If you go to the lawyers sooner you will both be taught to hate each other. This is the downside of Anglo-Saxon adversarial justice.'

Bianca replied, 'You don't understand what I want. I want to kick him where it hurts – *in the money!*' 'Funnily enough,' I said, 'what I am suggesting to you is a better arrangement than what you would get from the lawyers. You will be in a far stronger position if you can keep friendly relations going. Whereas you won't otherwise.'

She was simply not interested. My advice fell on very deaf ears, and, sure enough, things were extremely difficult after the divorce. Mick and Bianca could hardly bear to speak to each other, and when much later on their daughter, Jade, held an exhibition of her paintings, although they both attended the launch event they stood in opposite corners of the gallery. They were unable to treat each other civilly for years, nor to discuss the financial separation terms which were tougher on Bianca than mine would have been, and without which they most probably would have been able to maintain their friendship.

I had always appreciated the fact that Bianca was ravishingly pretty, and yet she often acted like a child if she was in company, in that way she had of appearing to dress entirely for herself, completely at odds with the overall tenor of the lunch or dinner party. It was obvious that this was a deliberate choice on her part, to shock or draw attention to herself. Conversations with Bianca at these events were always somewhat limited: she conveyed her thoughts in an odd blend of Spanish, a little French and semi-incomprehensible English.

However, away from social occasions she was quite different. When Josephine and I were on Mustique for Colin Tennant's fiftieth birthday party in 1977, long before we bought a house there, we were parked with Mick and Bianca at their villa. What Bianca enjoyed doing most was sitting chatting with the Spanish-speaking servants about the fish and other houschold affairs. There was also talk at the time that she was having an affair with Roddy Llewellyn, who was in Princess Margaret's entourage. She refuted this idea point blank. 'Non,' she said. 'Not even Haslam can have him!'

I had been at Steve Rubell's New York Studio 54, during its brief flare of fame – the club, on West 54th Street, lasted less than three years – on the night that Bianca was photographed on the back of a white horse at a party to celebrate her twenty-seventh birthday. Rather than riding the horse into the club as the subsequent urban legend always insisted, she pointed out that the horse was brought in as a surprise, and she briefly sat on it wearing a long red dress by Halston. The shot of that moment by the photographer Rose Hartman inadvertently fuelled the myth that she had appeared in the club like some latter-day Lady Godiva. She had, however, made an entrée into at least one event in Mustique on the back of Colin Tennant's pet elephant, Bupa.

Mick was now involved with Jerry Hall, who had become a major influence in particular on his attitude to the drink and drugs that were such a part of the early tours. Jerry cleverly told Mick that drink and drugs were extremely bad for his looks. He took this warning very seriously.

Despite all this upheaval, commercially the Stones were doing well. *Some Girls*, which had been released in the summer of 1978, proved to be their best-selling album ever in the States, although there had been a great deal of trouble getting it released. The title song's lyric included the line 'Black girls just wanna get fucked all night', which caused plenty of controversy, not surprisingly, with various organisations, including at one point Jesse Jackson's organisation PUSH (People United to Save Humanity) – although Mick always claimed that the song was meant to be parodying racist attitudes rather than purveying them. Atlantic Records, however, would not accept the line of the lyric, and specifically the word 'fucked' in that context.

Within the contract with Atlantic I had inserted a clause which said that if the company objected to a lyric, or to a cover artwork, and if we were unable to resolve the issue, the only solution would be for Atlantic to state that they refused to put the album out, in which case I had the right to go to another record company . . .

So I wrote a letter to Atlantic effectively saying, 'Pursuant to Clause x of our contract, I note that you have refused to put out the following lyric, and we hereby give you notice. I am enclosing a letter from Jerry Moss at A&M confirming that he is happy to put out the album for the same advance.' Ahmet Ertegun got on the phone with a degree of alacrity and he and I found a way round the problem, part of which involved Mick mumbling the words so quickly that it sounded like something else.

I was also getting set for a major change in my own life. Throughout the 1970s I had been continuing my work as a managing director of Leopold Joseph. By the end of 1980 I had made up my mind to leave the bank. Throughout the previous decade, I had still been working on other deals for the bank – a complex reconstruction of Fairey Aviation, for example, that had required frequent trips to Belgium, where the company was based – as well as looking after clients and attending board meetings at the bank which I could not miss.

In those days if you were a merchant banker you had to pay extremely close attention to what was happening in the bank, because as a partner you were personally responsible for the money. One was in it up to one's last suit of clothes. At the end of every day we checked whether we were long or short in the particular currencies we were dealing with and tried to close off that currency position each night: it was our money.

Only later, when banks no longer involved personal relationships with clients, did underlings start playing fast and loose,
speculating with other people's money.

Leaving Leopold Joseph was a difficult decision, because at
least I knew what my future might be in a small merchant
bank, and I realised that I probably had a successful career
ahead of me if I stayed. As things developed in the money
markets of the world during the next years, had I remained on
at the bank it would have been as remunerative or even more,
as we would have sold our little bank to a larger one. However,
that would have made me somebody else's employee, a prospect that did not appeal to me at all.

If I worked primarily with the Stones, I would be less
constrained by the demands of all the regular meetings. I
would no longer have to sit in on discussions about the rise of
the Deutschmark, or analyse what we should do about the yen
– although, that said, all of that experience was to prove enormously useful whenever we were planning world tours and
having to calculate what we should do about the currency
exposure. The years spent at Leopold Joseph had been of enormous value.

Above all, I was happy working with the Stones and rising
to all the challenges that the role offered. I think that was as
important a consideration in my mind as the fact that I also
knew I was going to make more money more quickly from the
band's touring activities.

My fellow directors at the bank were remarkably understanding. The official history of the bank suggests that there
were tensions and disagreements between me and other board
members, and differences of opinion over the future direction
of the bank. My recollection is somewhat different. We were

all great friends, and had been for many years, and they saw that it made sense for me to concentrate on my work with the Stones – and I am also sure that they were thinking quietly to themselves, 'Well, Rupert's share in the bank's profits will now come to us . . .'

So, in January 1981, I left Leopold Joseph to set up my own company, Rupert Loewenstein Ltd. On 6 January that year I made a note in an occasional journal I kept: 'My new career. Let us hope for the best. I am however so bored with Leopold Joseph that I want to see if I can achieve something on my own, in the business line.' Nine months later, on 15 September, I wrote, 'For some reason I have not been able to enter anything in this diary for nearly four months. Why? A delayed reaction to my change of job, I suppose. After all I have broken the habit of a lifetime – school – university – Bache – Leopold Joseph all being safe havens and now the plunge: a totally new career with only myself to rely on.'

Once I was out of the bank, it seemed as if I might be able to broaden my client base within the music industry beyond working solely with the Rolling Stones. I had previously had one other foray into the music industry with Cat Stevens, whose manager, Barry Krost, had been introduced to me by David Geffen.

Cat Stevens had a record contract with Jerry Moss at A&M which had been fulfilled by his current album, *Foreigner*. He had originally been signed to Decca before moving to A&M, where he had enjoyed great success with albums like *Tea For The Tillerman* and *Catch Bull At Four*. Barry Krost thought that his client might benefit from some help in drafting the right contract for a move to one of the major US labels, and David Geffen suggested that I might be the person to do it. So Barry and I worked to try and get Cat Stevens a better contract.

In the event those negotiations did not come to anything but I did manage to give Barry Krost some hints about touring, advise him about improving his touring contract and generally provide some financial thoughts to increase the income of Cat Stevens.

Later I was again involved with Barry and Stevens, when Stevens was in the process of moving towards Islam. Born Steven Georgiou – by birth he was half Greek-Cypriot and half Swedish – he had now chosen to change his name a second time and take the name Yusuf Islam. As a result of his religious conversion he grew nervous about his understanding of the tax situation, if he followed what he understood to be a ban on any interest he would receive on his money.

We had several rather difficult meetings about this, because one of the things we had done was to arrange for the bank to pay him a fixed, though higher, amount of money against his royalties for a longer period of time before he would enjoy the basic capital sum at the end of the period.

For one meeting, I was summoned to a meeting in Barry Krost's office in Curzon Street, in London's West End. When I arrived at the house, Cat Stevens took one look at my shoes and said, 'Weren't you told to take your shoes off?' So I said, 'Yes.' He raised an eyebrow. I continued, 'I see no reason why I should and I don't want to.'

During the meeting I told him, 'What you are trying to do is to get me to agree to pay you more money than we are giving you if you change from having this guarantee every year in the future. You fail to understand that the reason we can give you more is because we are using the interest. You are not.

And secondly even if you were there is no reason why you should give up money for which you already have signed for and negotiated.'

So he said, 'Well, you see, the Prophet, his name be blessed, doesn't really approve of music, although there is a moment when he hears Fatima play a pipe and he is moved by that.'

He then pointed out that the Prophet also approved of poetry, and that therefore he was thinking of putting out a book of his poems. Whereupon I said, 'Whatsoever the Prophet says, and whether he is blessed or not, that is your interpretation. In this conversation you must consider whether he wants to pay you a large amount of money for your recorded songs, which are very popular, rather than pay you large sums for your verses which have no public at all.'

At that point we ended our conversation and I left, half expecting that, had I removed my shoes as requested, they would shortly have followed me out of the door in short order and at high speed, aimed at my head.

After leaving Leopold Joseph the most significant other client in this period was Pink Floyd. I started off representing David Gilmour, the guitarist, and later negotiating the terms of the split between the band and Roger Waters. Waters was trying to wrest control of the group for himself, on the basis that he was the primary songwriter – and, indeed, it is fair to say that the album, show and film of *The Wall* was mainly his work in terms of songwriting, and the anti-military sentiment of *The Final Cut* had been very much about his father, who was killed on active service for Britain in the Second World War.

The main reason I was brought in was to examine a situation that had occurred with their manager, Steve O'Rourke.

Bernard Sheridan, who was the Pink Floyd's lawyer and a friend from LSE days of my partner Louis Heymann, told me that he thought David Gilmour was being taken for a ride and needed somebody to look after him. I made a note in my journal: 'London. Lunched with David Gilmour (not the young historian but the Pink Floyd guitarist) at Wiltons. He was, of course, late and I dreaded that he would be sent away as he was bound not to be wearing a tie. He arrived without a tie and with a garnish of stubble – looking like a lorry driver's mate – but was allowed in.'

One of the first things I noticed when I became David's adviser was the fact that Steve O'Rourke was charging David – and Nick Mason, the drummer – more commission than he did Roger Waters, which was unusual, to say the least. I felt that my job was to change that arrangement, which I did, but this, alas, complicated my relationship with Steve O'Rourke.

Steve O'Rourke was obsessed with being a creative manager – a mistake I was determined never to make – and he thought that Roger Waters was the key person in the band, which blurred his focus. I thought it was a great shame. I think an element of outside pragmatism was a help.

There was a battle royal over the rights to the name Pink Floyd. Roger Waters claimed that he was entitled to use the name. David Gilmour and Nick Mason had at least the advantage of greater numbers, especially when they had co-opted the keyboard player, Rick Wright, to join their faction. It took a lot of time. David Gilmour never bothered to overcome the dislike that he had for Roger Waters. I told him, 'It doesn't matter whether you like him or dislike him. You make a huge amount of money with him.' And there I failed. He just couldn't bear to work with Roger.

Roger had his office in Ruvigny Gardens near the Thames in Putney. When I went there it reminded me that my mother had had a house in the same street. One evening she was entertaining a group of friends and a burglar forced his way into the house and burst into a room where she and the friends were gathered. Caught off guard and faced with so many people, and my mother looking rather ferocious, he turned on his heels and ran out. My mother went after him, hooked him by the collar, and said, 'Come along, you'd better have a drink.' It turned out the miscreant lived in the same street, so she made a deal with him that he would look after the house whenever she was away, as a kind of informal personal security guard. That was typical of my mother's attitude to life.

That there was any prospect of resolving the impasse between the members of Pink Floyd was in no small part due to the fact that Roger Waters took on Peter Rudge as his manager. I had known Peter very well ever since he had been tour director for the Stones, and within the space of two meetings with Peter we had done a deal which satisfied both parties.

I got the Pink Floyd name into the hands of Gilmour and Mason. With Roger Waters now an ex-Floyd member and the three-man version back in action – although Rick Wright was retained only as a salaried sideman rather than a full partner – I was involved in their next tour, but before negotiations for a second got very far I had to go back to concentrating on the Rolling Stones.

I also had a brief involvement in the 1980s with Terence Trent D'Arby. The London MD of CBS, Paul Russell, contacted me and asked if I would consider taking Terence on as a client: they thought he had enormous potential, but, equally, said he was in a tremendous mess. There was a wonderful moment when I managed to persuade Mark Birley to allow this New York-born rock star, clad in black leather and chrome, into the urbane surroundings of Harry's Bar on South Audley Street. 'After all,' Mark observed with a smile, 'he does have a fine English aristocratic surname . . .' I was only involved in Terence's first album, *Introducing The Hardline*, from which he did very well. It turned out to be the last of my flirtations with other artists. The Rolling Stones were always my main concern.

By coincidence Leopold Joseph, after my departure, had retained a few music industry clients: Peters and Lee, Suzi Quatro and Smokie, but they never formed a major part of the bank's ongoing business. In 2004, after eighty-five years, the bank relinquished its independence and was acquired by the Bermudan bank N. T. Butterfield. Of the original consortium that Alexis de Redé and I had assembled in 1963 only Robin Herbert remained, having served the bank for longer even than Leopold Joseph.

By the time I left Leopold Joseph in 1981, the City was completely different from my first days there. When I had started, lunch was an essential part of the job, nothing was written down and by and large people trusted each other. By the early 1980s written data had become necessary and reciprocal trust had nearly disappeared: the revenge of the new world.

In that first year on my own in 1981 the primary focus in my work with the Rolling Stones was a major gamble as to whether the band would complete their US tour. Mick was not at all sure that he should. He was only persuaded, I think, by my impressing on him that if he did not do this tour the Rolling Stones would go out with a whimper rather than a bang – and also that there was a lot of cash to be picked up to pay for all the costs of his divorce from Bianca.

Of course his fear, when he got me over to New York in July to see the band during the filming of a promotional video clip for the new record, was that the rest of the band were, in his view, undisciplined, incompetent, unenthusiastic and incapable of the sustained work needed.

I pointed out to Keith, who had exactly the same fears about Mick and the other band members, that he was fixed in his 1960s King's Road time capsule and that what they felt they lacked in youth should be made up by discipline. Because, I said, without care, the band could have been seen as a frightening sight with no sense of preparation. But it must be remembered that an audience loves seeing trapeze artists perform without a net . . .

This was the beginning of an era when Mick and Keith really did not see eye to eye. Given the new stability in their private lives, one might have imagined a new maturity settling upon them, but the opposite occurred. One of the main factors was the issue of their solo work outside the Rolling Stones: Keith had released one album as a solo artist, and Bill Wyman had taken everyone by surprise by having a hit with his single '(Si, Si) Je suis un rock star'. Mick became very exercised about his own solo career.

Mick and I had long conversations about what he should do. I said that I thought the next album he did should be a solo release, so he could see how it went, and see how he made out without the band. If it was as successful financially as a Rolling Stones album, then obviously that would become an alternative option for him, to go it alone.

When the rest of the Stones heard about this, they were

naturally very disappointed since it looked as if they were just about to make significant money from the tours after all the changes we had put in place.

The differences were heightened because of other unilateral decisions Mick had made. In 1980 he had determined to get rid of Earl McGrath from his role as President of Rolling Stones Records. The way he set about this was by sabotaging all the plans that Atlantic and Earl had put in place, based on conversations he and Earl had had, which Mick then denied. What happened was precisely what Mick wanted to happen: Earl flounced in and gave his notice. I was very sad about it, because Earl was such a good person to have involved liaising over the cover designs, and had in fact been one of the few people who had been able to maintain good relations with both Mick and Keith, right up to the point that Mick decided in his own mind Earl was too much of 'Keith's man'.

Mick was consequently delighted when Earl handed in his notice. I had tried hard to convince Earl not to resign. 'Don't you realise the benefits you are enjoying, not only your wages but all the secretarial support? Mary at the next desk is arranging your travel, booking tables in the best restaurants, organising your life for you.' But Earl would not be swayed, left, and consequently life with Atlantic became much more difficult by several degrees.

Another area of difficulty concerned the role of Jane Rose, who had been the secretary to Peter Rudge at the time Peter was the Stones' creative manager and tour director. Jane then moved to work for Mick as a secretary, but after their working relationship ended, she subsequently moved to work with Keith and became his amanuensis. This was the kind of situation, perfectly normal in some ways, that could exacerbate any underlying tensions. It was a sign that things between Mick and Keith were moving towards a situation with all the destructive potential of the Roger Waters–David Gilmour relationship in Pink Floyd.

Things came alarmingly close to the edge of the precipice when we were negotiating terms for a new contract with CBS under Walter Yetnikoff in 1983. For a period the Stones had had two record companies: we wanted to return to a situation where one single record company handled them worldwide. Ahmet Ertegun at Atlantic was not prepared to make a high enough offer, which CBS *were* ready to deliver.

Matters were proceeding, I thought, in a positive direction. Walter Yetnikoff was highly professional, if irascible. He had started out as an attorney at CBS Records in the 1960s (we are almost exact contemporaries, I have discovered, as he was also born in August 1933) before becoming president in the mid-1970s and reinventing himself as a larger than life character. The title of his own memoir says everything about the reputation he wanted to convey: *Howling at the Moon: The Odyssey of a Monstrous Music Mogul in an Age of Excess*. His bad temper could flare up unexpectedly, which meant that one never quite knew what was going to happen in any discussion.

At a very advanced stage in these negotiations the band and I were staying at the Ritz in Paris – remarkably, in retrospect, since only very recently had the Stones even been allowed by the hotel management to be guests there.

A meeting was set up at the Ritz between ourselves, our lawyers and Walter Yetnikoff's team. This was intended to be nothing more than a rubber-stamping of everything that had been agreed in advance during the course of countless meetings. We had worked out all the small print and were, as far as

I was concerned, going through the formality and courtesy of taking the Stones through each element of the contract.

The meeting had been arranged for 6.30 or 7.00 in the evening, and the head of CBS Records in Paris had booked us into a grand, fashionable restaurant for dinner to mark the completion of the deal and to celebrate this new phase in the Stones' relationship with the record company, the role of good food in any business arrangement being taken much more seriously in Paris than in New York. A two-hour meeting, we thought, should be perfectly sufficient to run through everything.

When the Stones arrived it was obvious that they were all the worse for wear, including Charlie Watts. And, therefore, as we came to the clause concerning the deductions made for packaging costs or something normally of completely minimal interest to the band, Mick or Keith would suddenly cut in with, 'Whoa, well, I don't see why we should pay for *that*.' And so one had to explain, patiently, in what capacity this clause would be implemented, and how much money might be involved. 'Well, I don't understand that . . .' they'd moan. This happened with nearly every clause and became extremely irritating. They were showing off, simply messing around, but consequently messing both CBS and myself around. They were making no sense at all, of course. This tomfoolery went on and on and on. The meeting was going very badly.

Walter Yetnikoff asked for a break. He took me to one side and said without further ado, 'If this rubbish goes on, I'm calling the deal off. Unless we can get this arranged in the next ten minutes I am closing the relationship.' I realised that he was obviously concerned as to whether in the future he would constantly be having to deal with this sort of nonsense, and he was so irritated by the Stones' mindless nitpicking, purely for effect, that he was quite capable of tearing up the whole contract there and then. This was an extremely serious moment.

I asked Keith and Mick to come outside with me so we could have a little chat about this. As we came out of the Ritz they started laughing, sniggering like schoolboys – two very vociferous schoolboys. 'We just thought we'd get a bit of fun going.' As we walked around the Place Vendôme, I said, 'Well, the "fun" that you're having could result in you having no contract.'

With those few magic words, the pair sobered up almost immediately. 'Now,' I asked sternly, 'is everything going to be all right when we go in to the meeting again?' 'Yes, fine,' they said contritely. 'Your concerns are trivial. I want you to come back into the meeting, say that you are looking forward to the dinner and that you are sure that everything is under control.' The meeting reconvened, Mick said, 'Clause y is OK, and of course we understand that you will listen to our views, so we needn't have any differences about that.' It was hilarious ... And so the meeting passed off without incident. As did dinner. Disaster, for the time being, had been averted.

And thank goodness it had – not least from a commercial point of view. This was a period when the compact disc was in its very early days. And one contractual point which I had managed to achieve was to get the same percentage for CDs as we did on LPs. Walter Yetnikoff had not conceded that with any of his other artists: the record companies were trying to pay artists smaller percentages for CDs on the basis that this was an expensive new technology.

As I discussed this with our lawyers, I said, 'I tell you what we are going to do. We will say to him that we want the same percentage but that we are prepared to accept that the higher level only comes into effect when CDs represent 20 per cent or 25 per cent of the US market' – of course, it turned out that it didn't take very long for that to be the case.

Thankfully, we had not reached that particular clause in the contract before I was able to bring Mick and Keith back into line, because the Stones had not the faintest idea about what the really important elements were, and, if they had argued about the CD percentages, that small but significant victory would have been very difficult to reinsert into the deal.

At the time for me, that meeting had been a moment of annoyance over their lack of professionalism, frustration that the hours and days of detailed contractual negotiations might be undermined, and concern that Mick and Keith's *lack* of concern meant that they had given up on the idea of continuing as the Rolling Stones.

Now, as I reflect on that particular moment, it may well have represented a significant turning point after all the ructions and rifts between the two of them, as their schoolboy pranking in fact meant they were now feeling playful, and had rediscovered something of their old anti-authority, band of brothers spark.

That walk around the colonnades of the Place Vendôme in Paris was in a way a physical manifestation of my continuing relationship with them. How many times before had I – and afterwards would I – take them for a stroll around a virtual Place Vendôme, taking time out from all the excitement, alarums and shenanigans to try and interject a moment of calm consideration? It was the rock'n'roll equivalent – though substantially less lofty – of one of Aristotle's walks through the shady colonnades of the Lyceum in Athens.

I once described my role with the band as 'a combination of

bank manager, psychiatrist and nanny'. Above all my job was always to focus their minds on the true value and the commercial realities of a situation that could drastically affect their ability to achieve the two things that were most important to their existence as a band: continuing to make music together and earning their just deserts as a result.

With the CBS deal signed, for the time being the relationship between Mick and Keith was back in place, but underneath tensions were still bubbling and there was much more to come before they settled their differences.

9

'A lion is at liberty who can follow the laws
of his own nature'

R. H. Benson

With the CBS deal finally signed off in 1983 and a tempo-
rary, rather uneasy truce established between Mick and
Keith, there followed a phase of relative inactivity in the
Stones' endeavours as a group entity, certainly so far as going
out on the road was concerned. Their own solo projects
continued – as did the tours connected with those releases
– and a couple of Rolling Stones albums emerged. Behind
the scenes there was plenty of continuing work involved in
making sure the Stones' machinery churned from day to day.
The legal wrangles with Allen Klein also rumbled on, flaring
up from time to time.

However, this comparative hiatus in touring activity, coupled
with the fact that I was no longer tied into the demands of
working for Leopold Joseph, allowed me a hitherto unusual
freedom. Consequently I was able to devote a certain amount
of time to counterbalancing the work I had been doing in the

music business by tending to the more private side of my life. That side had been ever-present throughout, but, in general, I had tried to avoid it impacting on – or perhaps more accurately, being impacted *by* – my involvement with the sometimes godless world of rock'n'roll.

It was not, however, always possible to avoid such a clash. During one of their European tours the Stones were due to perform at a large outdoor show in Naples. Ever since I had become involved with the band I had always obtained their consent to donate a certain percentage of the profits of each tour to such charitable organisations as each of the band, myself and the tour promoter wished to support.

At the time of this particular tour I was the President of the British Association of the Sovereign Military Order of Malta (BASMOM), an ancient Catholic order founded nearly a thousand years earlier. In my capacity as President I wrote a letter directly to the Cardinal-Archbishop of Naples offering a donation at the end of the Stones' tour and asking for details of the right recipient, whereupon I received a brusque reply from the Cardinal to the effect that he refused any donation from the concert, saying he could not possibly accept such 'tainted' money as he was not prepared to sully the good reputation of the hierarchy in Naples by benefiting from the questionable moral values of the Rolling Stones . . .

I had a similar response from Catholic cardinals in two South American countries – and on a later tour in Argentina this tension even more strongly underlined by the fact that a section of the videos that the band had been using as part of the stage show showed crucifixes falling through the air. In this instance I brought myself to suggest to the band that this element should be amended or eliminated as this background imagery might well give offence. I was pleased to see that they did take notice of my advice and made some suitable alterations for the background videos at the shows in Buenos Aires.

There was always a delicate balance between the business and private halves of my life. I tried hard to work around the demands of both schedules, and we would plan for major family occasions to fall outside Stones tours if at all possible. There were times, though, when I could not go to a Stones event because of a private commitment having been entered into long before, and vice versa, usually for funerals, which of course could never be planned in advance. When I ever wondered 'Why wasn't I at that wedding or requiem?' I would then remember it was because I had been at a Stones concert.

In the same way, although religion has played an important part in my life I avoided the temptation of introducing my beliefs into my relationship with the Stones. Nor did I try and probe their own beliefs. Keith certainly would believe in a 'power', no doubt about that, and Mick, I would have thought, was the normal Christian. Do they distinguish between good and evil? Sometimes they do, sometimes they don't, but I don't think organised religion plays a significant role in any of their lives. Yet they always respected my own commitment and fully understood how important it was to me.

Only if we were entertaining in a primarily Catholic country would I have ever raised the point that their lyrics, or the staging – as with the flying crucifixes in Argentina – might be seen locally as either obscene or religiously insulting, and therefore that it would be foolish to include them, since taking them out temporarily would not materially affect the overall impact of the show.

As a committed Catholic, to be working so closely with the

Rolling Stones, a band who had recorded a song called 'Sympathy For The Devil' and released an album titled *Their Satanic Majesties Request*, might seem to pose a dilemma, but I always felt that the public perception of the band was somewhat skewed. In my journals I once wrote of Mick: 'The church however sees him as a purveyor of satanified obscenity, which is not so: the group has always been saucy but not satanic. A Halloween pumpkin satanism.'

Perhaps it is a characteristic of mine that I do not approve or disapprove of things very easily. If people behave extremely badly I do not immediately leap to any judgement – good or bad – of their actions, which is why, when my partners in Leopold Joseph said that they disapproved of the Rolling Stones' personal lives, I pointed out that many directors of important companies had precisely the same faults. What did anybody's private failings or preferences have to do with making money for them? Only if their activities threatened to lose money for the bank would we even attempt to intervene. 'We're not there as priests,' I told them. 'We are there as bank managers.'

When I was a stockbroker with Bache & Co., I had taken precisely the same stance. When people said that they did not wish to buy shares in companies which manufactured bombs or other weapons of destruction, I always told them, 'In so far as your financial life is concerned you should look at whether the company is successful in making money rather than how it does it. Don't judge the scenery from a murky pond.'

Catholicism was always part of my life. I knew that I was a Roman Catholic from as far back as I can remember, whatever 'being Roman Catholic' would have meant to a child of five or six. Some of my earliest memories are of Christmas, which in southern Germany is always celebrated on Christmas Eve, when the children are shown the tree surrounded by their presents, all gathered sing 'Stille Nacht', and then the adults go to church very late, once the children are in bed. Although we might have been living in Paris or London we always followed that German tradition, and I would have been taken to church every Sunday unless we were travelling.

My father, although he would call himself a Roman Catholic, was also much interested in Oriental religions and the Egyptian religions of the Pharaohs (an interest he shared with his brother Hubertus). My mother once said to him, 'It would be much better if you stayed a bad Catholic than became a good Egyptian.'

She had not forced Catholicism on me, however, and she had indeed sent me to St Christopher School where Quakerism was blended with the beliefs of the Theosophical Society – which had been founded in New York towards the end of the nineteenth century and at the time embraced a world of rein-carnation and high crankery – although, to be fair, the school authorities saw to it that I attended Sunday Mass and took instruction from the Catholic priest.

The most important influence on me occurred when I was studying in Cambridge at the age of sixteen. There I met Father Alfred Gilbey, the chaplain to the university. Mgr Gilbey – his father was a scion of the family of gin merchants – was my great hero. He had studied Modern History at Trinity College, Cambridge, attended the Beda College (sponsored by the bishops of England and Wales for older vocations to the priesthood) and became the Chaplain to Cambridge University in 1932.

Father Gilbey was very much a traditionalist and celebrated the old Catholic Mass throughout his life, for decades after the modern Mass had been universally adopted in 1965. He told a story that on his final visit to Rome, the then Pope sent word that Mgr Gilbey was invited to celebrate the new Mass, with the Pope as the only concelebrant, in St Peter's. He was highly amused by this – though naturally he accepted the invitation. Although he was concerned about the direction of the Church, Father Gilbey did not in any way attack the new Mass, and pointed out that the rite had changed half a dozen times since St Peter's time in Rome.

Cambridge only admitted female undergraduates as full members of the university after the Second World War – whereas Oxford had done so in 1920. Mgr Gilbey would refuse to act as chaplain for the women undergraduates, saying he had quite enough demands on his time looking after the male students. Yet he was exceptionally kind to undergraduates, and indeed exceptionally so to me, since I was not an under-graduate there.

I used to drop in to see him at the Catholic Chaplaincy in Fisher House on Guildhall Street in Cambridge. Indeed, I continued to visit him right up to his final, ninety-sixth, year, just before he left the Travellers Club in Pall Mall which had been his permanent base for over three happy decades after he stepped down from the chaplaincy at Cambridge, and where he had his own makeshift chapel on the top floor, in which he celebrated the old Mass.

While being tutored in Cambridge I had also encountered a very interesting Belgian Benedictine priest, Father Dominique de Grunne, who, like Mgr Gilbey, also lived well into his nineties, a lesson perhaps in the benefits of leading a priestly existence. Father de Grunne was a member of an old Catholic aristocratic family, and had become a Benedictine monk. However, he had not been happy as such and did not see eye to eye with the community of Maredsous, the important Benedictine abbey and monastery near Namur in Belgium, which he had entered.

After serving as a stretcher-bearer during the German invasion of Belgium in 1939 (during which campaign his father was killed in the fighting), he went to Switzerland to recover, and from there became the private tutor of the future King Baudouin of Belgium. By coincidence, many years later my son Rudolf was to teach Baudouin's own great-granddaughter.

He then came to Cambridge to study, having got to know Stephen Spender and, through the Spenders, the Darwins and the Cornfords. In 1952 he moved to Oxford. Hugh Trevor-Roper described the new arrival, who was doing the round of parties there, as 'charming, elegant, well-born, rich, handsome and intellectual', and as someone 'before whom all social doors have flown irresistibly open'. His charm and sociability led to him later becoming laicised, as he had a long liaison with the wife of a well-known author, a Catholic; she was separated from but still married to the writer.

Father de Grunne was indeed a highly intelligent man and I learnt much from him; we got on extremely well. He always said that if you view life and spirituality as a graph it doesn't matter if it goes up and down as long as the basic trend is upwards, which was a reassuring thought. His maxim, especially towards the end of his life, was 'pas de sentimentalité', a sage motto for anyone as they grow older.

By the time I went up to Oxford Catholicism was completely part of my life. I would have had long arguments with friends trying to persuade them of my views, the ordinary discussions of undergraduate life, disputes long into the night. I had theosophical doubts, what I believe is called 'theodicy', based on Leibniz: in other words, how do you make an all-loving and all-powerful God compatible with the existence in this world of evil? But these are the troubles which cross the mind of most people at some point in their life.

When Josephine and I had decided to get married, the fact that I was a Catholic and her father a diehard Ulsterman inevitably led to some friction. The Ulster Establishment could not bear the idea of Roman Catholicism in the same way that was evidenced by the German Baltic barons with their Lutheran faith in making their way in Russia (a notable exception was Count Alexander Benckendorff, Ambassador to London of the Tsar of Russia and a passionate Anglophile, who had converted to Catholicism from Lutheranism, and is the only lay person buried in Westminster Cathedral).

On one occasion when my future father-in-law, Montagu Lowry-Corry, and I were discussing the music for the wedding with the priest at the Brompton Oratory, the priest told him that a member of their priestly fraternity had been one Father Lowry-Corry, who was a great favourite. I saw my father-in-law squirm.

When Josephine converted to Catholicism a few months after our wedding, her father refused to speak to her for about a year, saying that none of his relations had ever been Catholic or even seen Catholics. I clearly remember overhearing him saying to a friend of his at dinner one night, a dinner at which we were all present, that they were 'lucky enough', even in Ireland, never to have had a Catholic servant – incredible, really.

My own children, like me, would have known that they were Roman Catholic from an early age. When we lived in Holland Villas Road, the house next door was a convent, and we would see our elder son, Rudolf, even as a seven- or eight-year-old, chatting to the nuns over the wall. He told one of the nuns, 'I know what I am going to do. I am going to grow up to be a priest and I will end up as Pope', by which she was extremely amused and which she relayed to Josephine. Rudolf indeed did become a priest – as also did my younger son, Konrad – though neither to date has, yet, been elevated to the papacy.

My daughter Dora has been involved with the Rolling Stones through her own PR and events company, and so the next generation represent both sides of my interests. I am sure that Dora must have frequently been frightfully annoyed by her two brothers appearing to be so pi . . . While she relished the opportunity to be part of a Stones tour, my impression was that Rudolf and Konrad were just as equally horrified by it and did not approve of my involvement with the band. However, Rudolf assures me that this is not true: he accepted that involvement as part of my work and although the world of rock'n'roll was not his particular 'scene', he trusted in my integrity and knew I would never do anything contra to faith or morals.

At one of the Stones' early concerts in London I had given them each six tickets. Out of her six tickets Dora ended up with eleven. Rudolf had only managed to 'get rid of one', so I gave his other five to Dora. Both boys were totally removed from rock music and the lifestyle. They loathed the music, in fact they didn't think it *was* music – but they had not realised, at least at that stage of their life, that they could convert their tickets into plover's eggs, rarities that others would covet.

Konrad is now a traditionalist priest in Venice, and brings to his work a stricter and more severe outlook on life than Rudolf, which I think comes from my father's side. Dora is a mixture: she has a practical side, which she gets from me, as well as an extremely kind side which I think comes from my mother.

I would not have ever seen myself becoming a priest although I could quite easily imagine having become a don, especially if I had had enough money to live comfortably as an academic, but the call of the priesthood was never strong enough to tempt me.

Rudolf's path to the priesthood was led by his interest in teaching, while Konrad arrived there via a flirtation with the law. He had always been very devout, but I believed was a more worldly person than his elder brother, and I thought he would enjoy the law. In his final term at Oxford I asked him whether he had considered a career and he said he had not really given it much thought. I said, 'Doesn't your tutor talk to you about that?' 'Did yours?' he asked. I agreed that he had never done so. Konrad said he would go and ask his tutor's advice.

When I next saw Konrad, he informed me, 'I saw my tutor, and told him that my father wants me to go into the law. So he sent me to see the law tutor. I went into the law tutor's reading room where there were huge tomes, massive Law Reports. The tutor told me, "Loewenstein, take out any of those books, open it at any page and read it out to me. Can you see yourself giving your life to that absolute rot?!"'

Despite the law tutor's lack of encouragement, Konrad

did nonetheless take his law exam in London and spent some time in chambers of a friend of ours, Mark Littman, a prominent arbitration lawyer. Konrad and Mark liked each other enormously and would have extraordinary discussions (as they still do now) during which Mark would believe he was going to convert Konrad to Judaism, and Konrad that he would convert Mark to Catholicism. After six months Konrad decided he did not want to continue with the law, saying, 'I've learnt that law is one thing, and justice is another.'

He then went to the University of Southern California to work for a Ph.D. in philosophy, while teaching alongside his studies. I thought he might enjoy the academic life, but eventually he told his mother that he intended to enter the Church and, when he talked to me about his decision, said, 'I know you're sad to know that you won't have any descendants with your name, but think of the prayers!' With Rudolf and Konrad entering the priesthood there would clearly be no direct male descendants in my branch, but in fact I was unperturbed by the news, because there were plenty of Loewenstein males in the other branches of the family, though mostly of a Catholic line.

Of course both my mother-in-law and my mother, for totally different reasons, would have been horrified at their grandsons going into the Church – my mother-in-law out of disapproval and lack of understanding of such an apparently foolish aberration; my mother because she would have thought that they were escaping from the world rather than living their lives to the full.

In June 2002 Konrad was ordained in Wigratzbad in the Fraternity of St Peter, established by a group of followers of

Mgr Lefebvre (the founder of the Society of St Pius X) who wished to return to full union with Rome. The Fraternity only follow the old rite in Latin and the old calendar. Konrad then celebrated his first Mass, a High Mass with wonderful music, in my mother's old home, Schloss Holzen, in a splendid white-and-gold baroque church.

It was most moving for me since, although my grandfather had sold it, the castle and the estate before the war, my mother and her forebears are all buried there.

Konrad's mode of priesthood is most impressive though occasionally inclined to be extremely rigorous. I once heard him preaching from the pulpit in the Church of St Louis en l'Isle in Paris – the occasion a High Solemn Requiem Mass for Baron Alexis de Redé, my partner in the Leopold Joseph consortium: the Mass was accompanied by Mozart's music performed by the Orchestre de Paris. I was in the front row with Mesdames Chirac and Pompidou and Monsieur and Madame Balladur. I wrote about it in a letter to my friend Jonathan Guinness: 'Konrad delivered a severe sermon from the pulpit. He went on to point out that all in the congregation would sooner or later die and some would go to Heaven and some would go to Hell; looking dramatically around he said that the only hope was to lead a good Christian life and he then concentrated on chastity, whereupon there was a tremor *dans le tout Paris* and Givenchy's aged companion passed out.'

In case I have given an overly stern portrait of Konrad, I should report that Rudolf managed to achieve the near impossible when preaching a homily for Josephine and my golden wedding: he made Konrad laugh out loud in church.

It reminds me of Robert 'Bertie' Swann, a friend from Oxford, telling me that one time when he was in Paris he had gone into Notre-Dame and to confession to an aged French priest. Bertie's French was somewhat halting, and the priest was obviously getting more and more interested in what was actually a very humdrum list of misdeeds. At the end the priest said to him 'Eh alors! Vous avez bien dit *l'inceste?*' When Bertie denied this the priest became very bored and a little irritated and gave him one Hail Mary as a penance.

There is also a story about one of the Catholic Loewensteins who had indeed been at one time Germany's 'senior Catholic layman'. It appeared that he was spotted coming out of a lady's bedroom (not his wife's) on his way to Mass in his private chapel at 7.00 a.m. A cousin of his raised an eyebrow, whereupon he explained, 'It's all right. I have already confessed.'

A natural progression for me in the 1980s was to become increasingly involved with Catholic charities. The first of these was the Order of Malta, the Roman Catholic Order of Chivalry of which my great-grandfather had been a member. The Order had originally been established in the eleventh century to protect Christian pilgrims en route to the Holy Land and the Crusades. Disbanded by Napoleon and ejected from Malta, the order was refounded in the nineteenth century as a charitable organisation specialising in setting up hospitals, clinics and care homes, helping the sick regardless of their own religion, which, however, included teaching them the faith.

The British hospital was originally founded at the time of the Crimean War by a rich Roman Catholic, who was also involved in the formation of the new British national association of the Order of Malta. The Order's sovereignty having been interrupted by Napoleon's invasion of Malta in 1798, Malta was then handed over to England in 1802 by the Treaty of Amiens with the stated intention of giving it back to the knights after the war. This never happened, however, because the knights made too feeble a representation at the Congress of Vienna and consequently Great Britain kept control of Malta until the era of Dom Mintoff. Some people say that the abandoning by the English of their promise to hand back Malta is the reason for the phrase 'perfide Albion'.

The Order kept going in Spain and Austria-Hungary and had retained its properties in Italy before, in the second half of the nineteenth century, setting up national associations in the main European countries. In England the Hospital of St John was therefore, in a way, partly founded by the Order at the same time as the National Association. To this day the Order's church is within the precincts of the Hospital, in St John's Wood, and all the publicity for the hospital concentrates on this historical past; indeed, it uses the Maltese Cross somewhat extravagantly. However, the Order has no actual power over the Hospital, except that it has the right to have two knights on the board and accounts for five of the fifty possible charity owners.

I was intrigued by a Roman Catholic order run not by the clergy – although the clergy provided spiritual comfort to the knights and patients – but by noblemen who had taken the three monastic vows. Friends of mine approached me and asked if I was interested in becoming a knight. I was, and since by then I had made a certain amount of money I was able to contribute to the good works of a worthy organisation. I was secretary-general from when I joined in 1981 for eight years, chancellor for six years, vice president for six years, and president for a further six years, twenty-six years in total.

I also became involved with ACN – Aid to the Church in

Need. This is a charity set up in the aftermath of the Second World War by a Dutchman, Father Werenfried van Straaten (his first name meaning 'warrior for peace'), initially to help German refugees from the eastern provinces left destitute by the war, and then expanded to help Christians around the world, especially in territories where they were being persecuted: by the Communists in the east of Europe, similarly in China and in the revived remains of the Ottoman Empire. Independently of my work with the ACN, Rudolf, during this time, was actively involved in smuggling bibles and other religious material to persecuted Christians in Eastern Europe, and was caught and interrogated on more than one occasion.

I was President of the British Association of the ACN from 1982 to 2006, and was able to bring a strong commercial focus to its operations, working to ensure that the UK became one of the top three fundraising countries. Working with the Order of Malta and the ACN has been a way of restoring some equilibrium to my life.

I make a regular trip to Lourdes to help with the pilgrimages there. It is such an odd place, a mixture of cheap hustling, of *bondieuseries*, pickpockets and sightseers alongside the real pilgrims. Many of those come regularly, either the sick in mind or body or their helpers, and many are helped greatly by the strong religious atmosphere and the fact that the sick give as much comfort to the healthy as vice versa.

The souvenirs on sale are often of the most astonishing and appalling taste: water bottles in the form of the Madonna with a detachable head, for example. I remember asking one of the souvenir shop owners how many of those items sold. 'Oh, much the most,' he said. 'Le bon goût fait rien à voir'. (An Italian friend of Dora's husband Manfredi once took the music industry's own Madonna to Mass at the Brompton Oratory and showed her the music of the creed which she sang impeccably at first sight.)

Mercifully, Eugénie-les-Bains is only an hour by taxi from Lourdes, and is the most attractive place to spend a quiet week or two: unspoilt countryside, very pretty house and wonderful food, *cuisine minceur*, which, when eaten, oddly enough decreases rather than increases one's weight. It was created there in the 1970s by Michel Guérard and his restaurant, Les Prés d'Eugénie, has maintained its three stars in the *Guide Michelin*, in which Eugénie-les-Bains is described as the 'Premier Village Minceur de la France'.

The Lourdes pilgrimages usually involve 250 or so of us, including fifty sick people, known as 'mallards' by the cheery helpers, their variation of 'malades'... The helpers are often either superannuated school children or bossy prefects (irrespective of their age), and sometimes can be quite wearing.

Dora, however, put it all into perspective by pointing out, one time when I was grumbling about a forthcoming stint, that it was no different from when I had to join a Rolling Stones tour and that the end of pilgrimage party, where many of the sick and some of the helpers do 'turns' and skits of their betters, could not possibly be worse than the Rolling Stones party that took place on a ferry plying between Denmark and Sweden where the bossy organiser tried to make me wear a Valkyrie's helmet and long peroxide plaits.

Father Gilbey came to Lourdes with us one year, and we were staying in the same hotel. Also in attendance was the Chaplain of the British Order of Malta, later Archbishop Couve de Murville. He was wearing a straw-coloured coat and collar, whereas Mgr Gilbey – like my son Konrad – only wore the traditional black soutane. He said to Mgr Couve de Murville, 'What do you think you are wearing here? I can assure you that St Bernadette would disapprove ...'

On medieval pilgrimages, I later learnt, pilgrims had to put up with repetitive, rather dull drumming, a constant quasi-musical noise all the time. Rock and roll has its precursors.

Rudolf learned to play the organ in church at the age of twelve and continues to play on and off. Konrad is also a good pianist and musically minded, and in his church in Venice he has wonderful polyphony as well as Gregorian chant. We were talking together about this and he said, 'You know, music is no longer a major part of my life at all. I'm not interested in it apart from Gregorian.' I said I couldn't understand that because he was very careful about the polyphony. 'Yes, of course,' he replied. 'That's part of what I'm doing.' But I could not imagine he was no longer impressed by the Mass in B minor by Bach.

At a point when I was involved in a number of large fund-raising galas for the Order of Malta, in conjunction with the Cirque du Soleil, I heard that Mel Gibson had financed the building of a small Catholic church in the Agoura Hills near Malibu, which celebrated morning Mass in Latin. As Josephine and I had a house in Los Angeles, I thought it would be interesting to see if he could be a sponsor of an Order of Malta event in London. I telephoned him, went over and had a long chat with him about the events and he agreed to become involved.

At the time Mel Gibson was about to release his film *The Passion of the Christ*. The Jewish lobbies were trying to stop its distribution since they objected to the Gospel's account, all written by Jews, about a Jew who was killed at the behest of other Jews.

He asked me if I would like to see an early version of the film, which was not yet completely finished. I said I would love to. And so I brought Mrs Nancy Reagan, Mrs Betsy Bloomingdale and Josephine along with me. We had a viewing on our own in his offices, which contained a large projection room. I then had further conversations with him about the film. Was he musically minded, I asked, because I had thought that Pasolini's film on Christ, *The Gospel According to St Matthew*, had been hugely influenced by using the St Matthew Passion. I told him that I had brought along a CD of the St Matthew Passion, as well as one of the St John Passion. 'If you'd put those in the film,' I suggested, 'It would lift the mood.'

I had discussed the film with my companions at the viewing and we had all come to that view that we had loved the film, and thought that the fact that it was spoken in Aramaic and Latin (but with English subtitles) was breathtaking. However, it seemed to us that it concentrated too much on the flagellation and too little on the Resurrection. I went a few times to Mass in Mel's church, but I was unable to persuade him to use the St John Passion, although he included some very good music at the beginning of the Mass.

When the Pope planned a visit to the UK in September 2010, the ecclesiastical organisers announced that they were going to hold three massive outdoor events: at Bellahouston Park outside Glasgow, in Hyde Park, and at Cofton Park in Birmingham, where he was to celebrate the beatification of Cardinal Newman, all at a cost of some millions of pounds. I suggested that if somebody like Michael Cohl, who had directed and marshalled all of the Rolling Stones tours from *Steel Wheels* onwards, was brought in, they would make money instead of having to pay it out, but they preferred for their own reasons – and inexplicably to me – loss to profit. *C'est la vie*.

On an earlier papal visit to Britain, I had attended the Mass celebrated by Pope John Paul II at Westminster Cathedral with half a dozen members of the Order of Malta. The notables and bigwigs at the Mass were being ushered by, amongst others, Alan Dunn and his brother Arnold, who ran the Stones' logistics and crew. Alan and I were amused that the Rolling Stones were, in a way, represented at such an event.

Through my involvement in both the Order of Malta and the ACN, I had been invited to two papal audiences, as part of large groups from both organisations. However, my first papal audience had been when I was far younger, in my early twenties. Travelling through Europe with my friend Michael Dormer (this was the trip when Michael and I encountered Baron Wrangell and his wife) I had packed a tailcoat since I knew Michael had arranged the audience in advance. He, in his early twenties, was already a Knight of Malta, and had been able to clear this through the British chargé d'affaires at the Vatican.

As it was high summer, the audience took place at Castel Gandolfo, the Pope's summer residence on the shores of Lake Albano, south-east of Rome. We were in a small group of half a dozen or so, and went through reception rooms one after the other, ever nearer the papal presence. We would be deposited in one antechamber and await a higher cleric to collect us and show us into another antechamber. Finally, after forty-five minutes or so, we found ourselves outside the room where the Pope, Pius XII, was waiting.

Once ushered in, we knelt in turn and kissed the Fisherman's

Ring. The Pope had been briefed about each of our back-grounds, and he talked to me in German (he was an extremely good linguist, and had served as Apostolic Nuncio to Germany in the 1920s); he knew some of my relations well. Five minutes later we were ushered back out. At the time the Pope was a figure of enormous mystique, compared to the global presence and celebrity of a John Paul II. Michael remembers that he was very tall and regal, and that kissing the ring was like kissing a block of ice.

The whole process of the audience, including the hierarchy of access, was in the back of my mind when we created the 'meet and greet' as a way of controlling all the people who wanted to meet the band on tour. The system of VIP passes allowed us to control not only who could get close to the band, but where they could go and, indeed, precisely how close. Those ultimately admitted to the inner sanctum would receive their five minutes' audience with the Stones, although for the corporate executives from the Midwest, rather than kissing the Fisherman's Ring they would be more likely to genuflect before Keith's silver skull's-head ring: a different kind of religion altogether.

5 July 1969, the Rolling Stones perform at a free concert in Hyde Park. Estimates of the audience ranged from a quarter of a million upwards. Mick opened the Stones' set with a tribute to Brian Jones, who had died on the night of our White Ball: Mick wore the same milkmaid's smock he had worn then.

Mick and Josephine during our stay at Warwick Castle in December 1969 with Lord and Lady Brooke.

Dominique Tarlé's photograph of Keith and Anita Pallenberg, with Gram and Gretchen Parsons, in Nellcôte, the villa they rented in the South of France during the 1971 recordings for *Exile On Main Street*.

Josephine en route to Mick and Bianca's wedding in St Tropez in May 1971; Stephen Stills is in the back seat.

From left to right: Ahmet Ertegun of Atlantic Records, Earl McGrath, myself, Mica Ertegun and David Geffen, Los Angeles, 1972.

Another increasingly rare moment of relaxation: with Josephine on a trip to Monchique, Portugal, 1972.

Patrick Lichfield's portrait of the Mustique regulars: HRH Princess Margaret reclining on the chaise longue, Colin Tennant brandishing a white cane. Josephine and I are sitting front left.

With Keith, doubtless debating the tax situation or overseas residency.

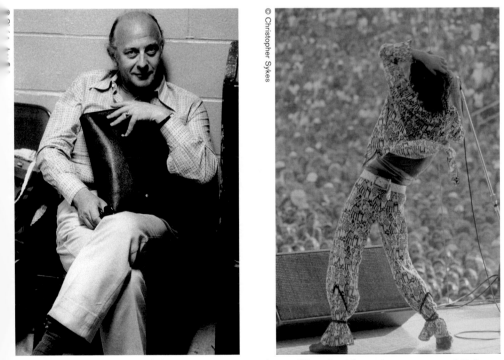

Backstage on the Tour of the Americas, in Jacksonville, Florida, 2 August 1975; Mick onstage during that show.

Dora marrying Count Manfredi della Gherardesca at the
Brompton Oratory, September 1998.

An audience with Pope John Paul II while attending the
General Council of ACN (Aid to the Church in Need)
in Rome in November 1987.

A family gathering in Castagneto in Tuscany for our
golden wedding in July 2007, *from left to right*: Father
Rudolf, Josephine, myself, Dora and the Rev. Konrad.

A portrait by Lawrence Mynott of me wearing the uniform of a Bailiff Grand Cross of Honour and Devotion of the Sovereign Military Order of Malta. Around my neck is the Grand Cross ribbon and badge of the Order of Malta, and over my shoulder the collar of the Illustrious Royal Order of Saint Januarius. I am also wearing the pale blue riband, and beside me are displayed the star and badge of a Bailiff Grand Cross of Justice of the Sacred Military Constantinian Order of Saint George.

With Josephine and our grandchildren, Aliotto and Margherita, photographed in the drawing room of our home, Petersham Lodge, in 2002.

31 March 2008. The lunch at Home House in Portman Square to mark my formal retirement from working with the Rolling Stones, Mick and Ronnie in attendance.

The photograph used on the invitation to the Home House lunch: a shot by Johnny Stiletto of Mick and me walking across Piccadilly.

10

'It is easier to forgive an enemy than to
forgive a friend'

William Blake

Despite having managed to pull Mick and Keith back from
the brink of sabotaging the deal with CBS in Paris in 1983, the
next phase in the life of the Rolling Stones was tenuous to say
the least. There was a strong possibility that as a functioning
unit the band might implode.

Mick was flexing his muscles, testing out his solo career by
releasing his first album, *She's The Boss*, in 1985. It came out a
few months before he appeared at Live Aid that July, performing in Philadelphia with Tina Turner, as well as on the video
of *Dancing In The Streets* with David Bowie. Keith and Ronnie
Wood did also put in an appearance in Philadelphia, as part of
Bob Dylan's band, but it was telling that the Stones as a band
did not perform together on the great 'global jukebox'.

This marked the beginning of what Keith has since dubbed
'World War III', a conflict that was to concern everyone who
was connected with and involved in the Stones. Ronnie has

said that he was worried that if Mick discovered that he was massively popular in his own right he might decide that he did not need the Rolling Stones as a vehicle – and, of course, as a solo artist Mick would have a much higher percentage of any proceeds from his solo album sales and touring. Keith in any case was unhappy with Mick's solo record deal, and doubtless shared Ronnie's fears.

Charlie was, in his own words, 'in a hell of a mess', having, to everyone's surprise, including his own, got himself mixed up in drugs in his forties and so was unable to act as an intermediary and go-between to help bridge the growing divide between Keith and Mick.

The band managed to put out one group studio album during this period, *Dirty Work*, which performed well, and included a hit single in 'Harlem Shuffle', but it also contained four tracks which had Ronnie's name on the credits, which he himself admitted was proof that the songwriting partnership of Mick and Keith, the creative mainspring that had driven the band since the 1960s, was not functioning at all well.

However, in the event, Mick's two solo albums – he also released *Primitive Cool* in 1987 – did not set the world on fire in the way he would have hoped. Maybe he did need the rest of the Rolling Stones after all.

Oddly enough, the person who in many ways helped to bring the Stones back together again, although he was intending to achieve exactly the opposite effect, was our old adversary Allen Klein. Since the original settlement which we had concluded following that all-night meeting with him in New York in 1973, the litigation between us and Klein had rumbled on and on, breaking out sporadically into intense flare-ups of legal activity, which created boxloads of paperwork as well as spiralling costs which helped line the pockets of the lawyers' expensive (and frequently brand-new) suits.

There had been four or five further settlements in the intervening years, and we were experiencing constant interference from Allen Klein, who said that he would not pay the royalties that were due and was generally making a major effort to disrupt any co-operation between the parties. By the late 1980s he was still twisting and dodging. I think he sensed, astute and as wily as ever, that the Stones were currently at their least cohesive point, and that they might well be ripe for tackling at the very time they were looking inwards to their own individual rather than communal interests.

It didn't work. Allen Klein certainly brought things to a head but succeeded only in drawing the band together, since I had to organise a number of meetings to discuss the latest flurry of legal matters with them. As Klein became once again the common enemy, it gave me an opportunity to spell out a few truths to the band, not least that Klein was far more dangerous than they had expected, given all the money and time spent litigating.

I was also able to reinforce an important message, which I now had the figures to back up: 'The way you make money is as a band. You have to do group work. That is what the world wants from you ...'

There was a band meeting in the Savoy Hotel in May 1988 that allowed us to work out the strategy for a seventh (and this time genuinely final) settlement with Klein in 1989. It also marked the beginning of the conversations between the Stones that led to the band reuniting at George Martin's AIR studio in Montserrat, and the pencilling in of a major tour to start in 1989.

It was clear once they got back together in the Caribbean, a part of the world which both Mick and Keith loved – apart from being a location with some taxation benefits – that they realised what fun they were having recording the new album and that they were once again creating satisfying music that they enjoyed just as much as their public.

It made me recognise that, although there had clearly been a lot of friction between Mick and Keith, it had been magnified and distorted because they simply had not been spending time together making music. Even during the recording of *Dirty Work* in Paris, I had had telephone calls from Alan Dunn in which he said that it was very difficult to get the two of them to turn up at the same time when the recording studio was booked and he was getting very concerned about what was going to happen to the album. That was a time when I had to speak to them separately and say, 'Look, you are risking throwing away a very remunerative contract, which is the last thing you want.'

The truth is that the pair of them were just going through a bad patch. These periodic problems can happen to all business partners. Mick and Keith, it must be remembered, had by this point been working together – and working *hard* together – for nearly twenty-five years, much of that spent under intense media scrutiny, constantly obliged to preserve their status with younger bands trying to challenge them and assume their mantle. In retrospect it was hardly surprising that they had a major wobble.

The bad temper and the remarks they made about each other – in private or to a third party – were a way of venting some steam. The whole process, Keith's 'World War III', in the end allowed them to emerge wiser, battle-hardened and with a much greater appreciation of what each of them and the other Stones brought to the group.

That said, there is a note I made in one of my tour journals in 1989 at the time the *Steel Wheels* tour had just got underway: 'The boys are back to scrapping, which perhaps they need. It is of course maddening for Mick that Keith is still addicted to the physical props of twenty years ago as well as the attitudes.' I remembered what one of my relations who dabbled in psychoanalysis had once told me. 'How right Uncle Werner was about Mick and Keith's trouble. His view was that a dispute like theirs – a form of divorce – is enormously complicated by being between two men each fighting to prove his male sexual dominance, whereas at least among a man and woman, or indeed a homosexual couple, that is usually clear.

'In a way Keith is coming out as the winner on a human level – Mick on a professional one. Alas! Keith is right and that is the problem. Mick has no real career which is to project his gigantic star quality, other than through his vast, and in my view, unique talent as a rock performer *with* Keith.'

Whenever problems did occur, I did not have to be unduly careful about worrying whether I was spending more time with Mick or Keith, which was fortunate as I probably saw more of Mick, especially when we both found ourselves together in Mustique. By and large this was not a big deal for Keith. He was certainly capable of losing his temper with me if he thought I was looking after Mick or the group without underlining his own essential importance, but otherwise he felt that my relationship with Mick was beneficial, maybe even necessary, in that there was somebody like me who had an independent influence on Mick. He knew that I would, like an ambassador, represent and articulate his views fairly to Mick.

I always found that, if I kept things on a business footing, it would diffuse much of the emotion. I did spend a great deal of time trying to eradicate emotion, just stating straightforwardly how and where they would make more money. Although Keith has described himself and Mick as a 'mom and pop' operation, they are not a married couple with a child. They are entertainers in a group. It nearly always comes down to a business decision.

There was one very embarrassing time when Mick wanted to have an extra remuneration on everything, on the basis that, in his view, he was the quasi-manager. I had a call from Keith a couple of hours later saying, 'Rupert, do you think that Mick's interventions in the things that you do make us money or lose us money?' I reassured him: 'I know what you mean – it won't happen.' But that proved to me that Keith knew what it was about, and could, if he did not succumb to a purely emotional response, deal with issues calmly and rationally.

Generally, when they were together in Montserrat, the work went smoothly. Even so, sometimes Keith could still not turn up until late or Mick might not be around when he was expected, and things could blow up off and on. Rather like the island's volcano, the recent eruptions continued to bubble up intermittently. But everyone in the entourage working with the band went out of their way to calm any moments of difficulty and ensure that the important business of making the album would continue.

While they were in Montserrat, Jerry Hall found herself in a potentially dreadful situation. She had asked for some suitcases to be sent over from Mustique via the airport in Barbados. Luckily she had not physically touched any of the suitcases, merely described them, because when the suitcases arrived they were found to be full of drugs. She was arrested and put into a jail in Barbados, which as a very good-looking blonde girl was not an ideal situation. She told me that she spent a terrifying night in prison with the Barbadian policemen slapping their thighs with their riding crops in a menacing way.

She had a very difficult time. I headed over there with the lawyers until it was revealed that this was all a (suit)case of mistaken identity. A porter in Barbados who was in league with the drug dealers in St Vincent had been off duty, and so somebody else had placed a drug parcel in her bags. Thank goodness she hadn't touched the luggage; had she done so, the ramifications could have been awful.

One of the key discussions during the recording was about the tour to follow the release of the new album, which was clearly going to be a major undertaking. I was scheduled to go out to Montserrat in a couple of weeks to talk about the tour with the band. Bill Graham, who had handled the previous tours, was the front-runner and had already made an offer of an advance.

I took a telephone call in the office one day. 'This is Michael Cohl. You won't know me, but I am a rock promoter. In fact I have promoted some of the Stones' dates in Canada on behalf of Bill Graham.' Michael said that Steve O'Rourke, the Pink Floyd manager, had suggested he call me. 'I've got a bid which I'd like to make to you.'

'Well, of course, you can do that,' I replied, 'but I have to tell you that we are on the verge of settling this with Bill Graham, so I am afraid you might find it won't work out because the sums we are being offered as advances really are significant.'

'Yes, I know,' said Michael Cohl, 'and I also know that he is prepared to pay you many millions of dollars. I am prepared to pay you twice as much.'

'Well, in that case ... we should certainly meet and talk about it.'

I contacted Mick and Keith as quickly as I could and told them that Michael Cohl was willing to pay a huge amount more. Naturally, they agreed we should consider his offer.

The discussions took place on Montserrat during a break in the recording, a series of meetings with the Stones and the lawyers, and separately with Bill Graham and Michael Cohl. At the end of the sessions I said to the band, 'I think you will agree that Michael comes out best.'

Mick, however, was concerned, as he always is, regardless of the monetary offer, with the scenery and production values. The principal negative in Michael's proposal was that he did not have the experience on the touring management side that Bill Graham had, since he had primarily been promoting concerts in his native Canada. Bill Graham, on the other hand, had within his team a number of people who were very strong on the staging side, in particular an Englishman, Mick Brigden, who understood décor and was able to translate and realise Mick Jagger's sometimes very complicated scenery ideas in a way with which Mick and Keith were perfectly happy.

In the event we decided that to offset this weakness in Michael Cohl's proposal we would bring in as specialists Peter Mensch and Cliff Burnstein, an 'odd couple' whose looks (Burnstein with the grey locks and beard of a hippie rabbi, Mensch's pate completely shaven) belied their abilities, not least that of being able to convince Mick that the show and the staging felt suitably contemporary, a form of reassurance he required.

We made our decision to go with Michael Cohl and informed the various parties. Bill Graham was furious. He found out which flight Mick was taking to New York, booked on the same plane and collared Mick. 'You're insane,' he shouted. 'Michael Cohl doesn't know how to produce. I've got Mick Brigden who's done all the last tours. The team all know you. What have you got against me?' Mick said, 'It's very simple, Bill: not enough money.'

Bill Graham later wrote, somewhat pungently, that 'losing the Stones was like watching my favourite lover become a whore'. He never even had the chance to pitch for any of the subsequent Stones tours: one October night in 1991 he died in a helicopter crash in the San Francisco Bay Area.

Michael Cohl worked with us on all the subsequent tours through the 1990s and into the 2000s. As I got to know him better I found that he was very bright, had great charm and was both unassuming and capable. Under his guidance the tour became the most financially successful rock tour up to that point: there was huge pressure on him and his team to deliver, since his advance had acquired the rights to handle not only the concerts, but also all the sponsorship, merchandising, radio, television and film exploitation.

The *Steel Wheels* tour – renamed *Urban Jungle* for the European leg – was on a suitably grand scale. The show was spectacular, the set like a huge power station on an odd distant planet: some kind of antediluvian Mars, I imagined.

The band were still able to deliver powerful performances. I noted in the tour journal I kept, 'At times their music is by and large so cacophonous, the crowd's enjoyment of it (when so many cannot hear or see the spectacle) still baffles me. Mass emotions both escape and frighten me.'

After one concert in the States, an American journalist delivered a review that, to me, was pretentious drivel. 'You might have thought,' I wrote, 'that he was thinking about Bartók, instead of what this is: rhythmic music with lyrics describing trite emotions. *But* it appeals to the millions. Why? Of course this show is stunning visually and has coherence from the point of view of that and the music. Also Mick has star quality as a performer that transcends the banality of the medium. But Bartók (or Bizet for that matter) it ain't!'

I was also struck by the band's choice of stage wear. Their garb was a rare motley: Charlie dapper as anything, wearing beautiful co-respondent shoes, cricket whites and a maroon waistcoat. Mick had a frogged open tailcoat and white tie (the 'faded aristo look', as Tony King, Mick's assistant and PR adviser, remarked). Keith and Ronnie affected black evening garments – a long black dress coat with medals and a bizarre form of dinner jacket like something found in a dressing-up chest at a country house for a modest charity event. Bill Wyman had a marmalade rinse and sports clothes, with acrylic turquoise accessories.

As the tour went round the world, some of the old issues were still concerning us. There was a point where there was a question mark over whether the band could perform in Japan. The money on offer was substantial but there remained some doubt as to whether they would be let in (due to Keith's and Ronnie's drug convictions) and how they would behave once they were there. A further drug offence, committed in Japan, would certainly land them in gaol and would seriously embarrass us all. In the event, we ended the tour with ten dates at the Tokyo Dome.

On these and other tours, I tried to maintain a balance with my regular life by seeing my old friends in any particular city the band were performing in. I would often introduce the Stones to those friends, which gave me an opportunity to counterbalance the meet and greets and the after-show parties with that instant rock'n'roll familiarity, where all the *perbeni* would be on instant first-name terms (disconcerting if one didn't want to be) and in open shirts.

One major change since the previous tours had been the pulling down of the Berlin Wall and the opening up of Eastern Europe. In Prague we were invited to attend a formal meeting with President Václav Havel. Prague was, of course, of staggering beauty – destroyed not by Anglo-American banks, only by the depredations of the Communists.

Earlier we had been to lunch in a pub that Havel apparently went to quite often to 'hear what the people think'. We were there with Karel Schwarzenberg, the Chancellor appointed by Havel, and a bunch of bearded artists and musicians. It really was Bohemian ... However, the conversation was somewhat stilted because of the language barrier. At the formal event President Havel gave an equally stilted and translated address accompanied by nervous smoking and attended by the Chancellor and three 'rock star' MPs. As I remarked to Mick, it was as though Mick ran a country with the band as MPs and with me in the Chancellor role. What an odd revolution.

During the European leg of the tour we had to cancel three nights at Wembley Stadium, including the final show to which all the VIPs were coming, because Keith had damaged his plucking hand. We substituted two of the shows later on, but perhaps Mick did not mind missing the third, since he always said that the English audiences were so inhibited they could only enjoy themselves in the dark, when they become anonymous – or unobserved – or when they are drunk.

Shortly afterwards we went to a party at Chatsworth House given by the Duke and Duchess of Devonshire for their grandson's eighteenth birthday. It was a marvel: some court-yards were tented over, some rooms open, including the private sitting room, but most of the rooms were *not* used. Even so, the 1,000 guests invited caused no crush at all, including 200 of their grandson's friends scrubbed and pink for their first ball, some arriving with rucksacks in time for a magnificent fireworks display given in the park to the sound of Beethoven's 9th Symphony.

During that tour we were in Italy while the 1990 World Cup was taking place. We had received advances from the Italian promoter based on a normal Stones sale, but that particular year ticket sales were noticeably down. We were not the only act affected: Madonna and Prince had suffered, too. I wondered whether it might indicate a change of fashion among the young, the tickets becoming too expensive and the seats in the higher tiers of a huge stadium too far away to enjoy the show. However, it seemed more likely to be a combination of other factors: the concerts falling rather too late in July, the fearsome heat, the holidays, Italia 90 and sorrow after the national team's defeat.

The situation had become so bad that the Italian promoter was trying to cancel the entire Italian leg, since he could not sell enough tickets to cover his outlay, and the guarantees we had shrewdly got him to give us, in England, before the shows.

Things were fraught: at one point the promoter raised the threat of arrest, saying the band's lyrics encouraged drug use, and telling us that because the drug laws in Italy had been tightened up, *proselitismo* (in other words incitement to use drugs) in front of an audience including persons under fourteen, carried a stiff prison sentence. Dora, my daughter, painstakingly copied out the lyrics in question and sent them over to a lawyer in Rome. She thought that 'You Can't Always Get What You Want' and 'Brown Sugar' were at risk ... after more than twenty years! It all turned out to be a storm in an espresso cup.

When we did turn up in Turin for the shows, never had I seen so many dope pushers as there were at the rather second-rate hotel we stayed in. I told Michael Cohl to tell the promoter to rid the hotel of all of them as a 'plant' would really be too much. *Carabinieri* did then appear, thank goodness. Just before the press conference there, Mick asked me, 'What on earth am I going to say about why we are playing Turin and Rome instead of Milan and Naples?' I said, 'It's very easy, Mick. You say they were also the capitals of the ancient monarchies ...'

The whole Italian saga ended in pure *opera buffa*. The promoter wanted us to pay him the rebate we had agreed on his guarantee before the trucks and stage left Italy. We wanted to pay the money only after they had left the country – as had been agreed in writing. There was a lot of hot air along the lines of 'You don't trust me, you doubt my word, you are terrible people, always contracts, contracts, here in Italy nothing is official'.

At 11.59 (we had to leave at midnight) I told Joe Rascoff, the tour accountant, who was livid with rage with the promoter, 'Joe, you will never hear me say this again, but pay them! We can't risk the equipment, or the people. Remember, there are young children in the tour party.' These weren't people we wanted to wrangle with. We paid the money, the wagons rolled and we escaped unscathed. The rest of the tour was a breeze by comparison.

After the tour, with the band having proved they were firmly back in business, we signed to a new record company, Richard Branson's Virgin Records. Richard reminded me that he had first tried to sign the Stones in 1975 when we were looking for a new distributor for Rolling Stones Records. He had indeed: at the time I didn't know him personally, but had certainly heard about him. He'd telephoned me and, although I was happy to listen to his pitch, I said that I thought the money would be more than he could afford, since at the time Virgin was still a small-scale operation, its one big hit being Mike Oldfield's *Tubular Bells*.

Richard was not at all fazed. Just as Michael Cohl did when we had a similar conversation, Richard told me he knew the situation, and that he would in fact offer significantly more than my estimate. I responded that since time was of the essence as we were very close to agreeing a deal, if he could show me a bank guarantee the following Monday we would definitely consider his offer seriously. I didn't think he would be able to get the money, so I was amazed when he turned up on the Monday morning, bank guarantee in hand. Virgin joined the auction, although in the end they were outbid by EMI, but Richard had proved to me that he was a gutsy young man.

Sixteen years later he finally achieved his wish when the Stones signed a three-album deal with Virgin in December 1991. One of the Stones did not sign the contracts: Bill Wyman was leaving the band after thirty years before the mast. He had decided, he said later, to get his personal life in order – he was coming to the end of his much publicised relationship with Mandy Smith, and wanted to start all over again, which he indeed did, settling down with a new wife, Suzanne Acosta, with whom he has three daughters.

I was looking for other ways of extending and supporting the commercial interests of the remaining Stones. Mick was diversifying into film making by setting up his film production company, Jagged Films. He had always dabbled in acting, of course: *Performance* was a good vehicle for him, because he was effectively playing himself, but when he played the lead role in *Ned Kelly* – he was filming in Australia at the time I telephoned him to say 'Drop Klein and go' – I did not think he looked like a great film star in the making.

I continued to hope, however, that I might find another film deal for him. I had lunch at Mark Birley's club one day in the late 1970s with Barry Spikings, who had won an Oscar as a co-producer of *The Deer Hunter*. A bottle of rather good champagne encouraged me to ask Barry whether, after his success with *The Deer Hunter*, he could see himself having Mick in a film. 'No,' Barry said, 'Mick isn't appropriate. Have you seen *Ned Kelly*?' I asked, 'What is it particularly that you don't like about his portrayal?' 'Well, Rupert, he can't project his voice.' 'But he projects his voice to hundreds of thousands of people on tour.' 'That's different. He's holding a mike. That's not the way you speak as an actor.'

In the 1970s actors still enunciated. I remember staying in Venice with Anna Maria Cicogna. John Gielgud was also a guest in her house and over the few days we chatted away. He said, 'The real thing is the voice training.' He reminded me of a TV documentary he had made during which he had been taken to RADA and asked for his views. 'It was so embarrassing for me, because I had to say, "You're well taught, but you're not taught how to speak." All that is going out.'

We also had an ongoing film drama with the IMAX company who, during the *Steel Wheels/Urban Jungle* tour, had shot a concert film called *Rolling Stones At The Max* to show on their vast screens. An early casualty of that project was the director, Bob Rafelson, who got on extremely well with Mick but for some reason not at all with IMAX. Consequently he was fired and IMAX decided to direct the film themselves. They were technically brilliant but slightly weird Canadians: the inventor only had seven fingers, which meant he had a somewhat disconcerting handshake. When we met I rather obviously patted him on the shoulder – luckily he was no Richard III.

The film world always had its own social norms. One day in Los Angeles I was taken to a glamorous, if tarnished, Hollywood film party where there was an excited gaggle of people gathered round a good-looking young man, whom I assumed was a star. It turned out that he was – a porn star. My host, Earl McGrath, in somewhat impressed tones, asked the young man how he managed his functions so well and for so long a time. His answer: 'I always have a stand-in for the insertion work . . .'

Away from Hollywood I was also seeking out new sponsorship and merchandising opportunities. We set up deals with Visa and Mastercard for cards with the Stones logo on, for example. But sometimes the best-laid plans would be scuppered. At one stage I had conversations with one of the top managing directors of General Motors who thought there might be an opportunity for an advertising campaign for a new car. The money being talked about was not in the millions but in the tens of millions, but Mick's opening comment was 'I can't see us being the lackeys of a big American corporation'.

Unfortunately the deal did not materialise since, when the proposal had to be endorsed by the three executives whose responsibility it was, it failed: they felt that the Stones were not able to approach the right age group. These were still early days for the advertising specialists to have such a close link with contemporary rock stars.

The problem was with the corporations. Phil Knight, the founder of Nike, who had made a huge fortune, was interested in a sponsorship involvement. He and his chief legal adviser came to my house in Los Angeles, where I also had one of our chief legal eagles. Phil Knight said he was prepared to agree to various conditions I was asking for, 'because all that we care about is our sportswear. And we think we could pay you . . .' he paused, '$250,000.' Given the exposure Nike would be getting if the band wore their clothes and shoes on tour, we didn't do the deal.

I continued to talk to potential partners throughout the 1990s. During one tour, a mutual friend suggested I should go and speak to Microsoft, who were looking for a jingle to launch one of their Windows operating systems. I took a plane from Los Angeles up to Seattle and was met at the aerodrome by a huge limousine driven by an equally huge black chauffeur who must have been six foot five with his chauffeur's cap perched on top of his hair, and mirrored dark glasses. As we drove towards the Microsoft headquarters, he asked me, 'You come from England, don't you? And you've just come up from

Los Angeles. What do you think of the OJ Simpson case?' The case was being re-examined at the time.

I was about to reply, when he interrupted, 'Before you answer, let me tell you something. I was a Black Panther, and I come from Georgia, where my parents' house was torched by the Klan. I think the outcome of the trial was a completely crooked verdict. It was a complete travesty of justice. The man was clearly guilty. All I am scared of is that you guys in Europe will think that American justice doesn't exist.'

He delivered me to the Microsoft offices. This time it was an American corporation of which the band clearly approved: 'Start Me Up' became the music that launched Windows 95.

11

'I must put my foot in a bit of truth, and
then I can fly free'

Andrew Wyeth

The decade from 1995 onwards marked a period of stability and
continuity for the Rolling Stones. On a regular cycle of two or
three years a studio album would be produced and a world tour
would follow. The Stones, now four in number with Bill having
departed, were supported by a set of sidemen musicians who
remained constant: Darryl Jones on bass, Chuck Leavell on
keyboards, a horn section based around Bobby Keys, who had
played the saxophone solo on 'Brown Sugar', and the backing
singers, Lisa Fischer, Bernard Fowler and Blondie Chaplin.

After all the machinations, upsets and alarms of the previous ten years, the Stones machine was purring along, to the
extent that each tour was, perhaps inevitably, becoming more
and more a *Best of* celebration, the most popular songs supple-
mented by a few numbers from whichever the new album was
and a solo set from Keith, before which he would remark that
it was a chance for the audience to go to the bar.

I asked Tim Rice to have a rummage through the Stones' back catalogue to see whether there might be an opportunity to create a stage musical out of Mick and Keith's string of hits, as Queen had done working with Ben Elton to create *We Will Rock You*. Tim came up with the idea of a musical about Machiavelli with the working title *Sympathy for the Devil*.

We got quite a long way into the project. Tim worked up a scenario and showed it to Cameron Mackintosh, who was interested, as I recall. I read the first draft and thought it could be great fun, but told Tim he would need to underline why Machiavelli might be thought of as being a devil, since not everyone would be as familiar with his work even if they knew the name. Without this being made clear, he would only emerge as a minor participant in a fascinating period of history. Then Mick objected to the whole enterprise: I think he had just finished another exhausting tour and did not want to head off into yet another intensive year or two putting on a musical. We shelved the idea.

This relative stability in terms of the band's touring and performing did not mean there were not other problems. Mick was coping with his long relationship with Jerry Hall.

Generally I tried never to preach to the band about their personal life. I didn't think it was my job: bank manager, yes, nanny, frequently, psychiatrist, on occasion, but relationship consultant, never. However, as it became obvious that Mick and Jerry were on the verge of splitting, I asked him if he really wanted to draw a line under their relationship, as it had clearly been so good for him. He said he did.

I switched from agony uncle to financial adviser. 'Do you want to pay her what now appears to be normal, even for a cohabitation?' He said yes. 'Fine. Firstly you have to stress that you didn't get married in Bali' – where he and Jerry had gone through a bizarre ceremony of sorts in 1990 – 'and that has to be made clear.' At the time the law was different in England and cohabiting gave no rights at all. I had to inform his lawyers of this and Mick pretended that this was a wicked scheme of mine, which it most certainly was not. Thankfully, he and Jerry reached an out-of-court settlement, since it would have taken a year or two to go through the courts, arguing over whether the Balinese ceremony was valid or not, with all the attendant strain and unpleasantness, appalling both for the parents and particularly for their four children.

Mick was a leopard whose spots never changed. During one tour, I had invited a friend who was a devoted Stones fan to come along with a group of his family and friends to the end-of-tour party at the Hôtel Georges V in Paris. During the course of the party I happened to notice Mick slide out of the proceedings and slip upstairs accompanied by my friend's attractive eighteen-year-old daughter. *Plus ça change.* When her father approached us, we rather timorously commiserated, but all he said was, 'Well done, daughter!'

A liaison with a longer-lasting impact occurred in Rio, when a very sociable young man, the son of another good friend, told me that he was planning to throw a party, which he wanted the Stones to attend, on a Good Friday. I told him, 'You can't have a party on Good Friday and have all the Stones fans screaming and shouting – what would your father think?' 'Oh,' he said, 'everything is very late in Brazil: it won't start until after midnight so it won't actually be Good Friday.' I said, 'No, but it will be Holy Saturday so that is not ideal either. In any case do what you want but I will not be there.'

Later I heard that Mick had gone to the party, met a very pretty and sweet girl there and nine months later she had a baby (Dora later told me that the little boy was, and is, very nice and good looking). At some point during the tour the singer Bryan Adams, who was performing as the support act and was a friend of the mother, saw Mick at a show, and said, 'I suppose congratulations are in order.' All part of the wonderful world of rock'n'roll.

I was reminded of a story about the late 10th Duke of Marlborough – known as 'Bert' – who was sued in a paternity suit by the wife of Captain Cunningham, who ran the Oyster Bar in Curzon Street to which we all used to go. Apparently Bert walked into his drawing room, threw down the newspaper in which it was reported and said to his wife, 'I really can't be bothered with this tiresome case.'

In the past there were many illegitimate children within the aristocracy. Usually they remained unrecognised and had to fend for themselves, since, in the words of Princess Liselotte of the Palatinate, the Duchesse d'Orléans, about her brother-in-law Louis XIV's illegitimate children, they were 'mouse-droppings', a reference to the expression 'mouse-droppings always want to mix with the pepper'. She was horrified when her own (legitimate) son wanted to marry one of the Sun King's (illegitimate) daughters. On hearing of the engagement she slapped her son's face in front of the entire court; the slap was reportedly heard 'several paces away'.

Of course attitudes can change. In my own case my forebear, Frederick I, Elector Palatine (the Victorious), legitimated his mouse-droppings, the first Counts of Loewenstein, by *matrimonium subsequens* which is what is required by Canon law; to be valid this requires both the parents to be free and to have been free to marry since the birth of the child, which was true in his case.

A lawyer friend of mine once passed comment on Mick's fecundity when we were discussing his separation from Jerry. He now had seven children by four different women, having only been married to one of them, Bianca. The lawyer's remark when we discussed the money that Mick had to give to the Brazilian boy was, 'Could you not teach your esteemed friend and client one simple word – "vasectomy"...?'

Even what had seemed to be a pretty durable marriage, Ronnie and Jo Wood's, foundered over Ronnie's very public relationship with an eighteen-year-old waitress, whom the papers delighted in describing as a 'Russian rose', although she spoke in perfect Estuary English. Not even Jo had been strong enough to keep Ronnie on the straight and narrow. This sparked a string of relationships with young women, whom Ronnie clearly saw as muses, since he said after splitting from one of them, 'I'm like Picasso, painting up the ladder after leaving his mistresses at the bottom after a row.'

My two sons having chosen to enter the priesthood, only my daughter, Dora, had the opportunity to make a church marriage, and in 1998 we celebrated her wedding at the Brompton Oratory, where Josephine and I had held ours. Her husband was Manfredi della Gherardesca, whose forebear Ugolino of Pisa's fate was recorded by Dante in *The Inferno* and subsequently relayed as part of Chaucer's *Monk's Tale*, so that was all to the good, and certainly better than a mention in *Hello!* (as opposed to *Hell!*).

In August 2000 Josephine and I became grandparents when Dora gave birth to a son. He was given the first name Aliotto, which Manfredi had discovered in the Gherardesca pedigree, a name which had been last borne by an ancestor of his who died in the early thirteenth century and was not a saint. That problem was solved by adding in a few more names, some of which were saints, including Rupert, since there was a St Rupert, Bishop of Salzburg, though he only had altars in the locality. At the time I remarked that Otto would make a convenient nickname in northern lands, while Alio would work, I supposed, in the West or the East flavoured with garlic.

Josephine and I were extremely happy at Aliotto's birth since our chances of descendants were so limited. My old friend Leo Ferdinand Henckel-Donnersmack had been very brusque about my concerns: 'since you have Loewenstein cousins with male descendants you have no concern as to what sex your grandchildren would belong to'. Aliotto's sister Margherita arrived two years later.

Shortly before Margherita was born we had been to Windsor for Princess Margaret's funeral. Johannes Thurn und Taxis once rightly said that funerals were preferable to weddings since by and large one knew whom one was going to see at funerals but nowadays one increasingly did not know whom one would see at weddings.

The 'tickets' for the funeral were rather strange since the women's, as well as the men's, said 'morning coat' or 'lounge suit'. If taken literally it would have made an excellent cabaret scene in the Weimar Republic. Also there was a flimsy note attached saying, 'You can get a cup of tea in St George's Hall after the service'. I did not think that David Ogilvy, the 12th Earl of Airlie, who was Lord Chamberlain to Queen Elizabeth The Queen Mother, would have allowed such wording to pass through under his white staff.

In Princess Margaret's later years Josephine and I had spent a week or so with her in Germany. Every other year we would go to stay with the odd relation and do some sightseeing. When we stayed in Coburg she was fascinated. When I asked her whether the Queen Mother had been there, she said, 'No, you see, Mummy never liked the Germans, because one of her brothers was killed in the First War and another was badly wounded.' Princess Margaret was very much at home in Germany and basically came to life as a German princess.

In Dresden, when being shown round the treasures of the Grünes Gewölbe, she noticed that the cipher of the Polish King Augustus the Strong, who founded the museum in the 1720s, was ARP: Augustus Rex Poloniae. She said to me in a stage whisper, 'Of course in the circumstances it might be tactless to explain to the Director what ARP means to us', remembering the air-raid precautions wardens who had bravely patrolled the city streets of Britain during the Luftwaffe bombing raids of the Second World War.

It was an elevation to the Establishment that caused another flurry of sparks to fly between Keith and Mick. Tony Blair decided to give Mick a knighthood, for services to the music industry.

I heard about the imminent knighthood from Jon Benjamin, who was in the Foreign Office. I first met Jon in 1988 when Mick was doing a solo show in Indonesia. I answered a knock on my hotel door in Jakarta and was amazed to find a small man with curly hair. I said, 'Morning', quite cautiously. 'Jon Benjamin, I'm second secretary at the embassy,' he announced. Up until then I still imagined that the British embassies were being run by the kind of gents with whom I was familiar. Jon was not at all part of old school tie network. He was stage-struck and found every possible way of helping us during our stay there. We made firm friends as he continued to climb the Foreign Office ladder, becoming British Ambassador to Chile in 2009.

After the call from Jon, I told Mick, who was secretly thrilled, but said in a nonchalant way, 'Well, I can't take the knighthood until the end of this Stones tour. We'll have to wait and see. I think next year would probably be better.' I called Jon Benjamin back and asked him what he thought about Mick's response. He said, 'The man's crazy. He'll never be offered anything again. He'll never get any help, nothing. He either takes it or refuses it, but we're not prepared to be played around with.' I rang Mick to tell him 'I'm afraid it's either take it or leave it', which he understood.

Then, of course, he had to deal with Keith's reaction. Keith was, not surprisingly, scornful. He called it a ludicrous honour considering the Establishment had thrown them both in jail, and came up with some wonderful bons mots, saying that he did not want to go on stage with someone wearing a coronet, and 'sporting the old ermine. It's not what the Stones is about.'

He declared it was a complete betrayal of everything the band had been. 'The idea of *Sir* Mick Jagger is grotesque,' he said. 'I've never heard of anything so absurd. Thank God I live in America!' He was absolutely furious. But the fact was that the knighthood was going to happen, so I could only try and calm him down. I don't think Charlie and Ronnie cared, but Keith really minded.

Later he mellowed and said he thought Mick should at least have held out for a peerage instead and become Lord Dartford. If a knighthood was ever offered to him, he said, he would 'tell them where to shove it'.

Keith has never shied away from delivering a pungent quote. During the *Bridges to Babylon* tour, in the immediate aftermath of Princess Diana's death in 1997, he was asked for his view on Elton John, and told the interviewer that Elton was a second-rate musician who had only become famous by writing about dead blondes ... to which Elton responded that he was not worried by the remarks of an arthritic monkey.

I had lunch with a Herald at the College of Arms, Sir Henry Paston-Bedingfield, who was also the genealogist of the British Association of the Order of Malta. I was looking forward to seeing him to discuss a suitable grant of arms for Mick: perhaps a cricket bat rampant and a guitar couchant, I thought. Sir Henry offered to show Mick around the College of Arms, but I knew that was the one thing Mick would not want: the news cameras would be there en masse and he absolutely would not wish to be seen, least of all by Keith, swanning around the College discussing the design of his knightly coat of arms.

For many people Mick's knighthood still seemed amazing, although the path had been prepared by Sirs Paul McCartney and Elton John, but it was not nearly as strange as some of the honours handed out. I can remember a time when the clubs of St James's Street seethed with rage about John Gielgud's knighthood and when the architectural historian James Lees-Milne was rumoured to be about to appear on the Honours List, a similar seething scuppered his chances. Mick's knighthood was another small triumph for heterosexuality in the arts world.

I tried to initiate one fine art project along the same lines as the portraits of Mick which Andy Warhol had created in 1975. This time my idea was to produce portraits of Michael Jackson.

I had a long chat with John Branca, Michael Jackson's lawyer, who came back and said that Michael would love to be involved. I then consulted Desmond Corcoran and Martin Summers of the Lefevre Fine Art gallery in London, and asked them who they considered to be the most prestigious portrait painter alive in America. They told me that in their view it was Andrew Wyeth.

So we arranged a meeting in the lovely house where Andrew Wyeth lived in Brandywine, Maryland. The estate was owned by an acquaintance of ours, George Weymouth, also a painter, known to everyone as 'Frolic' Weymouth. John Branca arrived, along with Wyeth's agent from New York. Michael Jackson brought with him his macrobiotic chef, a pimply young man from California dressed in a robe and turban, and a charming security man in his seventies, who had obviously been fulfilling that role since Michael had been a child.

During lunch Andrew Wyeth, who was getting along famously with Michael Jackson, said, 'You must work out what sort of costume you would like to wear for the portrait.' They were both costume freaks. Michael said, 'Oh, I think I'd like to wear a Civil War US Cavalry officer's uniform.' 'What an excellent idea,' said Wyeth. 'You must come up to my place by the sea in Maine and we will do the portrait up there.'

Andrew then asked Michael who his favourite painter was. 'Piero della Francesca,' he answered without missing a beat. I was so surprised I could have dropped my fork. 'Do you like the Impressionists?' Andrew continued. 'Yes, I do like them, but not Cézanne.' I was staggered by this interchange. Michael clearly had a highly educated approach to great painters, and was both talkative and charming, all in striking contrast to my expectations.

I was equally surprised when I asked Andrew Wyeth whether he had ever seen the Piero della Francesca paintings in some of the little churches in Italy, at Borgo Santo Sepolcro and Arezzo, absolutely lovely works of art which I had seen on a recent visit. He said, 'No, I have never been abroad.' I found it extraordinary that a world-renowned painter should never have been to Italy.

Alas, the project was stillborn. Wyeth's wife Betsy discovered that he had had an affair with Helga, the artist's great muse, and to pay him back she stopped him from doing the Michael Jackson portrait, which she knew he wanted to do. It would doubtless have been Wyeth's last major portrait since he died in January 2009. Michael Jackson – whom I had seen a few times after the visit to Brandywine, going to his concerts both in LA and London and chatting backstage; we got on well – died six months later.

Jon Benjamin and his Foreign Office colleagues continued to be of great help as we had new markets to tackle and I still saw to it that the Stones attended the embassy receptions in each country we visited. During the *Voodoo Lounge* tour of 1994–6, the British Ambassador in Buenos Aires, Sir Peter Hall, was delightful: he had been to Pembroke College, Cambridge, and was obviously highly civilised, notwithstanding him being a dedicated Stones fan. He persuaded us to call on the President of Argentina, Carlos Menem, which I got the band to do with no difficulty and the whole visit was a great success, especially compared to our previous problems in Argentina. The Argentinians who were camping outside the hotel screamed with hysteria like the wild fans of the 1960s and during the concert 800 had to be taken to the Red Cross tent, and 1,800 on the second night.

Our first attempt to appear in China, in 2003, had to be postponed. When news about the SARS epidemic first broke we were in Singapore, on the *Forty Licks* tour, and so I took myself off to the lovely British High Commission. Mick also called a few times to watch the cricket on the High Commissioner's television. We depended entirely on the advice from the Commission, and tried, as always, to balance the difficulties of commercial complications and moral imperatives.

I discussed the situation with Michael Cohl, the tour director. I kept Mick apprised of the state of play (of the SARS, not the cricket) from the first contact with the High Commission. The principal issue in this kind of situation was to discuss how, where and when we would be replaying the concert, whether it was a question of staying on a few more days or going somewhere else. If it was going to be difficult to find alternative dates in the gap we might need to do a couple of extra shows in Germany, for example. Mick was always very keen on not letting down the fans. There is no doubt that the Rolling Stones have always had a friendly respect for their fanbase.

We had never previously attempted to go into China when Mao Tse-tung was still in power because we had sufficient warnings from the Foreign Office in London not to bother trying. Unfortunately we did not have an equivalent of George St George, who had been so assiduous in helping me explore the possibility of performing in Russia in the 1970s. However, I did have some friends who were very powerful in Hong Kong, scions of British families that had provided the taipans, or business leaders, and I was able to seek their advice.

We finally made it to China in April 2006. In this country of over a billion people we only just managed to sell out 8,000 seats in the Shanghai Grand Stage, and most of those sales represented the expat community. We were still required to have all the song lyrics translated into Chinese for approval. I asked my daughter Dora to see whether or not they had followed the lyrics: she reported back that the translators had made them rather dull and, of course, cut out any tendentious moral laxity.

Nonetheless, the authorities asked the band not to perform a number of songs, including 'Brown Sugar' and 'Let's Spend The Night Together'. Keith suggested playing them as instrumentals, 'to give Mick a break', and Mick had a good line at the press conference, saying, 'I am pleased that the Ministry of Culture is protecting the morals of the expats and their girlfriends that are going to be coming.'

Although there were many tempting new venues and countries that wanted the Rolling Stones to perform there, the Stones always had such a large production to move around that, whenever we looked at the possibilities, the critical question was whether it could generate the appropriate income to make it worthwhile.

New opportunities opened up because of the change in world politics, in the footsteps of which rock'n'roll followed, never causing change to happen however much it might believe it did. Following the raising of the Iron Curtain, which had allowed the Stones to play in Prague during the *Urban Jungle* tour, the band went on in the 1990s to give debut concerts in Belgrade, Bucharest and Kiev after reaching Moscow, at last, in 1998, nearly thirty years after my first attempt (when the Russians I met knew the name of Mick Jagger but thought he was one of the Beatles).

The Stones performed in India for the first time in 2003, in

Bangalore and Mumbai, and experienced the usual confusion that awaits anyone doing business there. Our royalties in India were blocked in rupees but we were able to use those same rupees to buy air tickets, so we were able to justify the trip.

I had been to India back in 1970, when Josephine and I stayed for a few days with Her Highness the Maharani mother of Jodhpur who sent us to Jaisalmer for an outing with an overnight stay: it was some five hours distant over the desert. We were taken there by her personal ADC and stayed as guests of the local highness of this amazing state in the mountains made of yellow sandstone. I believe its main commercial interest was smuggling. His Highness received us in his braces in a large hall with a broken roof and broken silver furniture from the 1890s. He had glazed eyes and was surrounded by a few odd dogs and chickens and a startlingly good-looking ADC.

When we got back to Jodhpur Her Highness asked, 'What did you think of His Highness of Jaisalmer? I am afraid he has been somewhat ruined by drink and girls.' I said in as humble a voice as I could muster, 'I thought it was drugs and boys', whereupon she laughed loudly. The ADC who had taken us on the journey then took me aside and said, 'You see, Your Highness, in India we breed a special sub-caste who provide female concubines for some of the Princes and sometimes' – a little cough – 'young male attendants for the other ones.'

Mick had always been keen on playing in South Africa, interested as he was in the cricket. On the *Voodoo Lounge* tour it turned out that a visit to South Africa would fit in with one of the trips we were making to the Far East. We heard from the South African promoter that they were expecting 100,000 people at Ellis Park in Johannesburg.

I said to Mick, 'How many black people do you think will be in that audience of a hundred thousand? Apart from anyone in the touring company, that is.' Mick looked a bit bewildered, and said, 'Well, a decent amount, I expect.' 'More than five hundred?' He looked amazed, so I said, 'Do you want a bet on that?' We had a small bet and I think in the event the number was only a hundred. This was February 1995, five years after the release of Nelson Mandela. Changing deep-rooted social divisions can still be extraordinarily slow.

12

'When you can spend your life doing something
you love, you are living a very fine life'

Ahmet Ertegun

In late 2006 Ahmet Ertegun gave a dinner party for us in
New York, two weeks before the Stones were to play at the
Beacon Theatre in New York, a venue where Martin Scorsese
would be filming the performance for his documentary *Shine
a Light*.

I asked Ahmet whether he and his wife, Mica, would like to
come along. He said yes, so they joined our party. We headed to
the backstage area which, unlike the rest of the theatre, had not
yet been fully restored. There were rather large stone stairs but no
banisters. For once, nobody had really taken a good look at the
backstage area, apart from setting out some tables and organising the catering. We sat down at a table and had some drinks.

Ahmet said he would go to the lavatory. Mica asked him if
she should come too since the stairs were steep and Ahmet,
now in his early eighties, was quite frail. But he said he would
be all right. Nonetheless, Josephine said she needed to accom-
pany him anyway, so they headed off down this rather scary

staircase. When Josephine came out of the lavatory she told Ahmet she had noticed that the lock on the door was not working. He said he didn't mind.

He walked in and a couple of minutes later had what we think must have been a short blackout. In normal circumstances he would have slumped back against the door, but this time there was nothing to catch him. As the door was unlocked, it flew open as he fell backwards and he hit an unforgiving stone floor with the back of his neck.

Although we had the very good Rolling Stones doctor on hand we immediately contacted Ahmet's own doctor: an ambulance came quickly and took him to a hospital. The concert – in true show business tradition – went on, as Ahmet would doubtless have insisted. He never recovered from the effects of the fall, and died in hospital a few weeks later.

Ahmet had been a partner – and occasionally a sparring partner – throughout my Rolling Stones activities for over thirty-five years. In the early days his deep knowledge of the record business, especially in America, and the advice that he gave me based on that experience, had been invaluable – one of his maxims was that 'the music business is not just music, it's also business'. His sudden and so unexpected loss was a hard and deeply sad blow.

Earlier that year I had a health scare. In January I had a bad cough, which saw me wheezing away, making a sound rather like a small provincial symphony orchestra tuning up. I missed the Stones' free concert given on Copacabana beach in Rio the following month: nobody has yet managed to work out how many people were actually there: the lowest estimate was one and a half million, the highest two million. It was rumoured that the police came to an arrangement with the local gangs whereby, in return for peace, the police would not look too hard at the commerce that was being carried out in the audience.

Then I had a major haemorrhage due to diverticulitis which occurred in Tokyo and then later again in Shanghai. Luckily Brad Connor, the excellent New York doctor we had on the tour, specialised in the problems of medicine in some of our more out of the way destinations; it was he who finally told us not to perform in 2003 because of the SARS outbreak. His contacts were first class and I received immediate treatment in the best hospitals in Tokyo and then Shanghai, where I had a blood transfusion, and so I now have quite a bit of Chinese blood circulating through my veins.

Keith had also had a medical trauma that year. Following one Australasian section of the tour – which, in the light of what happened, was prophetically called *A Bigger Bang* – he, with some friends, went to a very expensive holiday resort in Fiji where he was foolishly tempted to climb a palm tree. Although from my perspective Keith was still comparatively young, he was not quite able to stay in the tree and so fell off it – but felt all right afterwards. Two or three days later he went water-skiing and fell down, as a result of which he had a severe headache. It transpired that a blood clot had formed between his skull and brain which had to be operated on in Auckland: he needed a good month of monitoring and convalescence. This meant that the tour could only resume after the cancellation of a concert in St Petersburg, to which I had been looking forward, since I was sure that it would be most glamorous; how odd, I thought, that glamour has died out in the West but perhaps might arise in the East.

Not surprisingly in the light of these events, the question of the effect of the passing of the years was uppermost in my mind.

Charlie Watts had been diagnosed with cancer of the throat. As well as his palm-tree accident and the damage to his plucking finger in 1990 (he nicked it on the end of a guitar string and it had turned septic), Keith had also fallen off a ladder in the library of his home in Connecticut a few years earlier. Mick lost his voice periodically: however, Peter Pan-like he might appear, the stresses and strains of singing on tour inevitably took their toll.

Bob Taylor, our insurance representative, said to me after one concert had to be cancelled, 'Well, we may have to put Mick on the Pavarotti pile.' 'What's the Pavarotti pile?' 'With Pavarotti we only insure three performances at a go.' I said, 'But you can't do that with the Stones, because they've had to spend millions just setting up the production. That has to be amortised by eight or ten shows.' Bob said, 'I know, that's what I am telling you. It's very dangerous, because a man in his fifties is going to lose his voice at some point.'

I had been thinking about how to address the question of the band's future for some time. When I turned seventy, I had told them, 'I shall have to start thinking about retiring, and I shall try to set up a system which is good enough to keep you with good advisers.' I could not see the Rolling Stones being able to manage more than one or two more tours of the magnitude of their previous global circumnavigations, which lasted a great deal of time and used up a huge amount of energy. I did not know whether they would be ready, willing and able to continue at that kind of level of work and interest.

The strain of the concerts was enormous: they could never do more than three a week. One side of the touring experience was that they had to give their all to different places, in different languages, on top of the demands of travel and the concern of the customs in so many different jurisdictions. I also felt that Mick would become increasingly anxious about whether he would be able to handle any diminution in his physical powers and therefore of his own performances, which had been superlative for so long: he can cope with what he is very good at, but not with anything he feels might be risky for his voice or his movements.

It was not only the levels of physical fitness, which could never be as high as they were when they were younger: touring is very hard physical work. The tours were also psychologically demanding because the performers were pushing themselves in front of hundreds of thousands of people and always dealing with criticism as well as adulation, including criticism of them continuing to perform as they got older: the 'Strolling Bones' jibe. Time was not on anyone's side. In fact, it seemed to be going faster and faster. John Gielgud, towards the end of his life, remarked that breakfast seemed to be occurring every ten minutes.

It had already become apparent that record sales were going to represent a far less important source of money for a rock band because of piracy and the beginning of the age when the supply of music was moving to digital platforms, with the advent of iTunes, MP3s and downloads, all of which we had spotted a long time before.

The rock industry business model would have to be altered radically, and future earnings from recordings for any band more difficult to predict. It would be much harder for the average musical talent to make a lot of money unless they were interesting performers although they would have much more work to do with jingles in the commercial sphere and sponsorship and film music. The Rolling Stones were not average, but even with their exceptional musical talent they were going to be affected by the same problems, and more besides.

If touring would be the primary source of income, and if Rolling Stones tours were going to become less frequent and more difficult, if not peter out entirely, then there was considerable uncertainty ahead, and my aim had always been to minimise uncertainty.

This lay behind various previous attempts I had made to find a suitable and long-term business solution. As early as 1997, in a journal entry from the *Bridges to Babylon* tour, I noted in the course of one day a morning meeting in New York with Michael Stone, the founder of the brand licensing company Beanstalk, whose clients included Coca-Cola ('very bright,' I wrote, 'and probably the right man to help in my venture of launching an RS corporation'). This was followed by lunch with Tommy Hilfiger at his factory: 'most able, *selon moi*, and very active: again perhaps the right man'.

I was examining potential purchases as well. One emerged from our previous work with IMAX. An opportunity arose for us – meaning Michael Cohl and myself, on our own behalf or in conjunction with the band – to buy IMAX for $25 million. We looked into this extremely carefully but in the end I, wearing an old-fashioned banking hat, said we couldn't afford it because the future earnings did not look certain enough.

By the early 2000s a position had been reached whereby an organisation within the peripheries of the entertainment industry was prepared to discuss a 'takeover' of the Rolling Stones. The deal would have produced a substantial amount of money for the band, but importantly the creative originality of the Stones' activities would not have been hampered in any way, with no loss of creative freedom at all. In fact in my view they would have gained greater freedom to finance any sensible projects they wanted to undertake.

The idea of this new, and to me eminently sensible, proposal was that the acquisition of the Rolling Stones by this interested party would have represented a huge plum in his corporate box, because the individual concerned was due to be taken over in turn by another company in a reverse takeover. Not only would there be a huge amount of cash down, particularly appealing in the period after the bursting of the dotcom bubble, but we would have additionally received the uplift that he would have received on his sale, should he sell the company for certain levels of money, which would have in part also been payable to us.

I thought the Stones could be taken over and each receive a significant tranche of money which was probably more than they would earn if they carried on, and they would still have other interests to keep them occupied, busy and amused.

This potential liberation represented the fruits of extensive conversations, negotiations and careful positioning, but I could not make any further progress without convincing all the band.

It was a frustratingly protracted discussion. I had innumerable conversations about the benefits of the deal through the whole of one tour and half of another. At one meeting everything was agreed, then at the next we were back at square one. Progress was painfully slow as we pirouetted through a series of seemingly never-ending volte-faces. I thought that one reason the band might be concerned about the deal was that they thought it would make them look as though they were selling out. The selling out one could have explained away by saying it was just a question of executives taking on a new partner, that no significant change had taken place.

I wrote to my close friend Lord Moyne, a former partner at Leopold Joseph, confiding my concerns: 'I have been living through very difficult times in my business life since I have found a staggering proposal for my dear rock clients whereby they would have been paid at least double, if not treble, what they might be worth if there was no appropriate buyer. But the transaction may now not take place at all and a decades-old business relationship will be irreparably damaged. What a to-do! Of course it may all work out; I am sure Micawber would think so!'

Finally, I made it clear to the band that we had to complete it by the end of one particular September, because the takeover was due to be announced in the autumn and the mechanics of that required the deal with the Stones to have been initiated.

Michael Cohl and I had a talk with Keith, who seemed to understand everything perfectly, and the following day we convened a meeting of the clans in my hotel room, the clans in question being Mick, Keith, Charlie and Ronnie, with the lawyer I had found for Charlie (his lawyer had already told me, 'Don't show me the documents, just show me the cheque', since it was so patently a good deal and a vast amount of money) as well as our own tax lawyer, who had drafted all the documents, and two other American lawyers.

Just as the meeting was about to start I took a telephone call from the person I had suggested to Mick as his private lawyer. He said, 'The deal's off. Mick doesn't want to do it.' 'Well, all I can say,' I replied, 'is that that is total folly.' Although I was personally sad that they were turning down such a spectacular opportunity, we had to carry on with the meeting as planned.

During the meeting Keith suddenly started shouting at me. I said, 'Keith, let's go next door and talk about what you want to say. There is no point in manifesting your bad temper in front of everybody else.'

Off we went, and I said, 'This is most unfortunate. You agreed with everything yesterday. What's all this about?' Keith was most disturbed, almost on the verge of tears. 'Don't you realise how terrible this is? It's our baby going away.' 'It is not your baby going away,' I said sternly. 'You are not losing control, as you fear, of your creativity. All you are ensuring is the safeguarding of a large sum of money which will in fact increase it.'

When we went back into the meeting Mick said, 'Well, you know, I'm not saying I'm absolutely against it. I mean, perhaps we could talk it over.' I was firm with him. 'No, Mick, the deal was that we had to come to the decision today. We have talked it over endlessly and spent months drafting and redrafting this document. Time has run out. We all knew that if we did not agree at this meeting, an additional, valuable sum would no longer be payable.' And in addition, I reminded him, we had asked a major Wall Street investment bank for their opinion and they had greatly endorsed the move.

Whereupon for the next six months Mick kept on trying to redo the deal. But it really was too late. That was one of the factors that precipitated my departure.

It made me realise that, from my point of view, after more than thirty-five years, things might nearly be over between me and the Rolling Stones. I was now old enough, in my seventies, not to be bothered with yet more toing and froing issues that, to me at least, seemed to be completely obvious decisions.

There had been many times when their behaviour in meetings amused rather than depressed me. Once, in the late 1980s, I had managed to get the band together for a meeting in a hotel in Washington, DC. This, of course, was an era when things were particularly fraught. I could see, as everybody else could, that Keith was getting increasingly fed up with the discussion, and clearly thought this interruption to his time quite unnecessary. He finally said, 'I am going to take a leak.' The meeting continued but I saw his eyes light up when he saw a large window that happened to be open. He sauntered over, and before one could say 'Jack Robinson' was peeing out of the window – luckily the canopy leading to the hotel lobby was directly underneath. I think I was the only person in the meeting whose eyeline he was in, since nobody else seemed to notice.

As far as the takeover deal was concerned, whatever the rights and wrongs on both sides – and naturally I believed that the route I had suggested was the right course of action – our views were too divergent. I was very frustrated because I felt that the Stones were coming home to harbour and that I had gone out of my way to organise a very agreeable homecoming, with double their net worth in cash in their pocket. They had decided not to take my advice and it seemed to me that we were now no longer thinking about business with like minds as we had done for so many years previously.

I made my mind up, set a date for my departure and announced it in March 2007. I would continue for a further twelve months, so that I had time to leave everything in as good an order as I could, and then gracefully withdraw. I felt some satisfaction that at least I had been able to help change the direction of the music business from its state in the first days of my involvement and to make it more organised and honest. Nowadays we see how important financial probity is in every sort of business and in a small way I had seen to it that that happened in rock'n'roll.

I made sure the Stones had good and experienced lawyers advising them on most aspects of the business alongside their own personal advisers. I told them that, if and when (at the time I feared it was more if than when, but hoped I was wrong) they came to put another tour together, they could find an additional team on an *ad hoc* basis to work with the lawyers.

The day I retired from working formally for the Rolling Stones, 31 March 2008, was marked by a luncheon they gave for me at Home House in Portman Square. Christopher Gibbs, who had first made the introduction to Mick back in 1968, and therefore had set the voyage underway, could not be there, but sent a message from Africa to say that he was 'sad not to be part of the beano to celebrate one of the most successful and glorious culture clashes of our times'.

Mick picked up on that notion of culture clash, remembering that in 1968 'we came from slightly different backgrounds. At the beginning of our relationship the great problem we had was "we got no money". And like the old saw that there is nothing as inevitable as death and taxes, Rupert did not promise that death would be avoided but taxes should certainly be legally minimised . . .'

Alan Dunn, one of the most loyal of the Stones' long-serving entourage, who had been in charge of logistics and the tour office, recalled that in the early days he had asked me what the future held, as what lay ahead was uncharted territory. I had replied with the words of Winston Churchill: 'I have nothing to offer you, Alan, but blood, toil, sweat and tears.' For his speech at the leaving lunch Alan had picked a quote to offer back to me, the opening lines of John Dryden's 'Happy the Man': 'Happy the man, and happy he alone, He, who can call today his own: He who, secure within, can say, Tomorrow do thy worst, for I have lived today.'

Although my day-to-day involvement with the Stones had come to an end, I remained concerned about how the four of them would move ahead. Without me, or somebody like me, working closely with them all and on behalf of them all, but not tied to any one individual, I thought it would be very difficult for them to act coherently, especially since Mick had always liked to manage himself, which was one of the things that brought Keith against him. If I was leaving the ship I wanted it to sail on. Despite the fact it would be heading into undoubtedly choppier and shallower waters, I had no wish to see it founder.

I left my office in King Street in St James's, where I had been happily installed for over twenty years, a location I much enjoyed since I was next door to Christie's and within easy walking distance of my clubs and the restaurants which had been my regular places for lunch. I decided to give myself a year's trial to see whether I could land any investment management business sufficient to cover the overheads. If not, Josephine would have to put up with the fact that, whereas in the past we had been married for good times and bad, but not for lunch, in the future lunch might have to be included.

At the time, I wrote, 'I shall no longer be looking after the investment management of the Holy Rollers which has been fun and rewarding and indeed very successful for nearly forty years . . . I am still not at all sure as to whether I would get bored if I didn't have some remunerative work, since it has been so much a part of my life for so long, but on the other hand the irritation and anxiety that I increasingly experience might diminish if I tried to get used to leisure. Was this not how Aristotle defined leisure: "the energetic pursuit of happiness"?'

Shortly after stepping back from the Stones, my term as President of the British Association of the Sovereign Military Order of Malta also came to an end on St John's Day, 24 June 2008 (having been elected exactly six years earlier), and with it the rather onerous workload that I had been undertaking for the Order, because not only had the role of president taken up a lot of my time, since the buck stopped with me, but I was involved with the powers that be in Rome.

Each November I would preside over an Order of Malta dinner with around 200 guests. In 2002 attending that dinner had meant me missing, to my chagrin, the Rolling Stones playing at a businessman's sixtieth birthday event: altogether, including his charitable donation, he spent more than $10 million on the evening. An amusing record, I imagined, although the great feasts and festivals of earlier days were comparatively more lavish and expensive.

The spectacular collapse of Lehman Brothers in September 2008 underlined the fact that this was a period of great change and turmoil. In the old days stupidity and greed on a large scale, or, indeed, true economic disasters, were geographically limited, and the international ones usually arose in those countries that were affected by war. But now the banks were going bust by lending money to people who could not pay it back.

I remembered a time when I went over to Basle to pay a call on the Bank for International Settlements, whose manager was an old-fashioned, one-armed Englishman who had been seconded by the Bank of England to manage it. During our chat we talked about gold and I probably, being young and brash, commented adversely on it for the usual reasons that it was a mineral whose quantity depended on mining so consequently one did not know its 'real' value, and in addition it paid no income. He looked at me pityingly and said, 'Young man, gold has provided a key symbol as the repository of wealth for hundreds if not thousands of years and it is likely to maintain this for many hundreds of years after both you and I have been and gone.'

My aunt Helga, then in her late eighties, had rung me after the collapse of Baring's in 1995, at 7.30 in the morning, saying two things: 'Firstly now, no English merchant bank, if Baring's go bust, is creditworthy? Correct! Secondly, I hear the Rolling Stones will be playing in Köln next week. Since they have made money for the family I feel that I should hear them before I die.' I got her the tickets and after the concert she was interviewed on German TV and asked whether they had been too loud for her, to which she answered, 'No, I am deaf.' Then she was asked what she thought of them and she said, 'Psychologically most interesting.'

I concurred, then as now, with her assessment, and applauded her attitude. I enjoyed around four decades of interest, not only psychological, thanks to the Rolling Stones. Although I had firmly resisted changing my own habits to those of the rock'n'roll business – music industry executives were constantly surprised that I could neither drive nor type and that I had never been to the Hard Rock Café. Well, there you are! Our father's house has many mansions – my life had certainly been enriched.

Epilogue

'Eheu fugaces, Postume, Postume, labuntur anni'
(Alas, the fleeting years glide by, Postumus,
Postumus)

Horace

During the long, highly entertaining, often amusing but odd marriage between the Rolling Stones and me, I have often reflected generally on why I do not and did not like their music. To many outsiders it must seem extraordinary that I was never a fan of the Stones' music, or indeed of rock'n'roll in general.

Yet I feel that precisely because I was not a fan, desperate to hang out in the studio and share in the secret alchemy of their creative processes (something I never did since I couldn't take the noise levels), I was able to view the band and what they produced calmly, dispassionately, maybe even clinically – though never without an affinity and affection for them as people. When it comes to matters of business, I have always found that calm dispassion is essential.

What puzzled me was what I thought about the Stones as musicians. They were certainly always very hard working with their musical instruments. There is no doubt that Keith in particular was obsessed over which guitar he was using, and the actual sound that he was producing. So, in so far as one is concerned with the way sounds which mean something are written, it must be called music.

When Mick was with friends of mine and brought out his guitar to play it, all the young people sat around absolutely loving it, while to me it was not a patch on a French guitarist I had heard playing at a nightclub and who had moved me far more than Mick did singing in a room. What was it that I found so different? Why was I out of step with popular, or populist, opinion?

Many friends were proud and happy recipients of gratis CDs; I never played a Stones track by choice. Josephine enjoyed their music more than I did, because of her dancing career, but, again, would never put on a Rolling Stones album. I have sat backstage through countless shows on tour, sometimes even out in the audience. Depending on who was with me I would stay longer if they were friends of mine who I knew were enjoying themselves. Despite that constant exposure I was never a convert. My personal tastes did not waver.

At one stage I even thought it was not music, but a pointless arrangement of sound with which I could not be bothered, but I came to realise that this could not be true, because the Stones' music has a great effect – greater than I ever thought – on the audiences. There is something in their use of sound that impresses people and that they like. People whose judgement in most matters I respected and trusted – Ahmet Ertegun and Earl McGrath, for example – also loved rock'n'roll. I would discuss this with them, asking them what it was that they found so moving in it.

I remember arguing about this once with the tour promoter Michael Cohl and Joe Rascoff, the tour accountant. They were saying, 'There is no such thing as generically good music or generically bad music.' I said, 'That's because in music you don't believe in right and wrong . . . and better and worse. But you do in other areas. You are very keen on good restaurants and you hate bad restaurants. Now all those restaurants are still producing and cooking basic ingredients which are served and then eaten. In some restaurants, you'll say, "This is absolutely wonderful", in others that you can't even eat it.'

I continued, 'And sometimes you don't mind going to a very expensive restaurant with bad food because the ambience and the waiters and the service are all very good, and maybe you can order some very good wine to go with the meal. In many ways it is an interesting method of calculation.'

So what do I mean by good music and bad music? Am I able to define it? Otherwise it is like saying, 'I don't like beetroot'. The Rolling Stones to me are like sausages and mash. Comfort food. In medieval times it was the pipe and drum, apparently dull as ditchwater. There is a note from one of my tour journals from 1990: 'Dora tells me that the agonising thumping music with the non-stop talking is a form of music called "Rap". Tense music in a synthesised squawk accompanied by odd shrieks and psychedelic effects. Half an hour of torment . . .'

One of my doctors, a very clever man, told me that there has been a study on music and depression, which concluded that there is a part of the brain which makes people who listen to Gregorian music happy and helps their depression lift; the same effect happens listening to Buddhist chanting. This part of the brain is affected by different sounds in different orders.

The doctor went on to say that at the congress in Kyoto where he had learnt this, there was a performance by Kodo drummers who played for an hour. He said it had an extraordinary effect on everybody: a sort of euphoria.

Research in the field of neuroscience, notably by Professor Antonio Damasio, of the Brain and Creativity Institute at the University of Southern California, continues to explore the link between the brain, music and emotion. There is a paradox in the fact that incredibly complex music written by composers and performed by the most technically gifted of musicians can not only be enjoyed by people who have absolutely no knowledge of music, but produces strong emotions in them, across many different cultures.

It seems that music enters the body in a rather primitive way, through the bones of the ear and the membrane of the tympanum (a drum, of course), and then arrives in the brain at the level where emotions and feelings are processed. Perhaps this explains some of the emotional impact of rock'n'roll, dominated by the rhythm of the drums and the physical impact of the bass pumped through ever more powerful sound systems.

Some Rolling Stones songs I did find moving. I enjoyed 'Paint It Black', for example. But by and large it was rather like the circus. When one stops being a child the circus becomes a bit of a bore and it requires a Cirque du Soleil to shake up the whole concept of a circus to make it once again a fascinating and intriguing entertainment for adults.

So when the Stones came on the stage, what did interest me was the performance, the backdrops and videos, everything that Mick was very good at doing and which created part of the magic of the show, and something which Keith was not at all interested in. He could never understand why so much money was spent on the production. His view was, 'We play better in a nightclub and the music has more meaning.'

The element of the performance, I felt, was essential. The charisma that could control a crowd was a powerful force. I once noticed that when Mick was not concentrating and going through his movements on stage he included what looked like some of the Royal Canadian Air Force gymnastic exercises which his trainer had probably introduced him to. People were cheering him doing that. I thought it unbelievable that doing some bending and moving your arms up and down impressed people. Clearly, from his dancing and the gestures, a huge amount of obsessional gratification was brought into being.

At one stadium in Munich I headed up to the very highest tiers and found a couple perched there before the show was due to start. I asked them why they were there. 'To see the Stones.' 'But you can't hear them and you can't see them from here.' To which they replied, 'It's still wonderful.' They were moved by the event, even though they could not say exactly what it was that moved them.

I have to say that Mick has a refreshingly honest and realistic view of the limitations of what he writes. After Andy Warhol had produced his set of prints featuring Mick, I suggested to Mick that a further option, which would be cheaper, would be to produce a calligraphic book using his lyrics, printed on wonderful paper, with illustrations. Mick said, 'No, no, no, my lyrics couldn't take it.' I was very impressed with his saying that.

The classical music that moves me has to be appropriate for the environment. Keith gave a birthday party during one of the European tours. He mentioned to me that he had brought along the CD of Richard Strauss's 'Four Last Songs', as he had recently seen it performed. 'I thought we might play it,' he said, so I advised him, 'It simply won't work with this audience.' He saw my point.

When our house in California was being built, the man in charge was Armenian: he stayed there with his pregnant wife and told me that she was only interested in classical music, listened to it very frequently and felt that it was good for the embryo. Josephine now has an upright piano in the house which she plays every day we are there. For a time a small bird used to come and dance to Mozart, but to no other music. We all respond to music in our individual ways. *Chacun à son goût* indeed.

Appendix: The ancestry of
Rupert zu Loewenstein-Wertheim-Freudenberg
by Guy Sainty

The Loewenstein-Wertheim family is the senior branch of one of Europe's oldest reigning families. It not only produced ruling Dukes, then Electors and Kings of Bavaria, but two Holy Roman Emperors, the first King of independent Greece, Electors of the Palatinate, Kings of Sweden, Hungary, Norway and Denmark and two 'anti-Kings' of Bohemia, who challenged the Habsburg kings in the seventeenth and eighteenth centuries.

They also inherited the Duchies of Julich and Berg which straddle what is now the German-Dutch border, the Counties of Holland, Hainault and Zeeland in what is now a large part of the Netherlands and Belgium as well as other smaller German states. The family produced a notable branch of the British royal family, of which Prince Rupert of the Rhine, Duke of Cumberland, is the best-known member, and a branch of the Spanish royal family (in the twentieth century). The Loewensteins themselves were minor sovereigns as rulers of the 'immediate' County of Wertheim and other smaller territories held as fiefs of the Empire.

Bavaria, the Palatinate and the County of Wertheim were all states of the Holy Roman Empire of the German Nation, founded on Christmas Day 800 when Pope Leo III crowned Charlemagne *Imperator Romanorum*. In 1512, this was formally titled the *Imperium Romanum Sacrum Nationis Germanicæ* (translated in German as the *Heiliges Römisches Reich Deutscher Nation*), or Holy Roman Empire, which is how this strange construct has been known to history and which was famously dismissed by Voltaire as being neither Holy, nor Roman nor an Empire.

In 1362 the right to elect the Emperor was defined and limited to seven ruling princes, three ecclesiastical – the Archbishops of Mainz, Trier and Cologne – and four lay: the King of Bohemia (who although an elector was otherwise excluded from the affairs of the Empire), the Count Palatine of the Rhine (Wittelsbach), the Duke of Saxony (Wettin) and the Margrave of Brandenburg (Hohenzollern). These were later augmented by the elevation of Bavaria and the Duchy of Brunswick-Lüneburg (as Hannover) to Electorates.

The Dukes, Margraves, Landgraves, Princes, and Imperial Counts, Barons and Knights, as well as the ecclesiasts who held 'immediate' territories, all enjoyed membership in the Imperial Diet, a kind of supra-national Parliament for the German states. This included the sovereigns of the larger territories such as Saxony, Bavaria and Brandenburg as well as the rulers of quite modest territories, or representatives of groups of statelets along with the Archbishops, Bishops, Abbots and Abbesses who ruled the ecclesiastical states. Considerable prestige became attached to possession of even a relatively modest immediate territory, some having only a few hundred inhabitants, and it was a measure of the standing of the Loewensteins that they remained immediate sovereigns until the Empire's dissolution in 1806.

The Loewenstein family descends from Berthold, Margrave in Bavaria, who died in 980 and whose probable grandson, Otto, acquired the castle and county of Scheyern, exchanged for that of Wittlesbach, a small township north of Munich, by the latter's son Otto II, in 1119. In 1214 the family also acquired the enormously wealthy County Palatine of the Rhine in 1214 and the duchy of Bavaria was ceded to a junior line. When the senior, Palatine, line became extinct in 1777 Bavaria and the Palatinate with the family's others possessions were combined into one state. In 1805, after an agreement with the French by which certain of the family's possessions along the left bank of the Rhine were ceded to Napoleon, Bavaria became a kingdom, remaining such until 1918 when the family finally ceased to reign.

The origins of the Loewenstein (in German, Löwenstein) branch go back to the marriage of Elector Palatine Friedrich I, who had become Elector on the death of his elder brother Ludwig IV, mortally wounded in battle in 1449 at the age of twenty-five. As he lay dying Ludwig commanded his brother Friedrich to support his young son Philip as his youth necessitated a regency. Since a regency may have required imperial permission, Friedrich instead assumed the title of Elector under the terms of an 'Arrogation' in which he undertook not to marry and, although the Emperor tried to intervene, Friedrich proved an adept ruler whose victory over the imperial allies at the Battle of Seckenheim in 1462 secured his own rule and possession of the Palatinate for his nephew, whom he had formally adopted in 1451.

Friedrich, however, wanted to marry his long-term mistress, Klara Tott (otherwise known as Klara Dettin), who had already given birth to their two sons a decade earlier; she was a former maid of honour at the Munich court and the daughter of an Augsburg burgher but not considered of suitably elevated rank to be the bride of a sovereign ruler. Philip, by then aged twenty-one, wanted to protect his own inheritance but nonetheless agreed that the earlier 'Arrogation' should be varied to permit his uncle's marriage, while excluding Friedrich's descendants from succeeding as ruler.

Friedrich married sometime before October 1471 with his nephew's consent and, on 24 January 1472, renounced his succession rights to the Palatinate for himself, his wife and their descendants. Friedrich and Klara's marriage served to legitimise them under canon law, since neither was under any legal impediment to marry once Philip had given his consent; furthermore, their two sons had already been legitimatised by bulls issued by both the Pope and the Bishop of Speyer before 14 October 1470.

The future Elector Philip must have recognised that he ultimately owed his throne to his uncle Friedrich, and it would have been ungracious for him to have withheld consent, particularly since Friedrich had not only defended his existing inheritance but had managed to enlarge it. Klara's elder son Friedrich, who died aged thirteen in 1474, and Louis (1463–1524), were accorded several properties and substantial sums but Friedrich died on 12 December 1475 before the grant of further estates could be effected.

Philip initially only allowed Ludwig, Friedrich's surviving son, the lordship of Scharffeneck (in 1476) and the County of Loewenstein (in 1488) but then, in 1490, granted his cousin the lordships of Abstatt and castle Wildeck and in 1494 asked the Emperor, Maximilian I, to raise Ludwig to the rank of Count of the Empire as Count of Loewenstein. Of Ludwig's five sons, only the youngest, Friedrich (1502–41), left descendants, of whom the elder, Wolfgang (1527–71), left an only son,

Wolfgang II (1555–96), who received the lordship of Scharffeneck and was known as the Count of Loewenstein-Scharffeneck; this branch became extinct in 1633 when the property reverted to the junior Loewenstein line.

Friedrich's younger son, Ludwig III (1530–1611), who had embraced the reformed Protestant faith, made a brilliant marriage in 1566 to Countess Anne of Stolberg; she inherited the lordship of Rochefort (a fief held jointly by the Prince-Bishop of Liège and the Duchy of Luxembourg), in what is now Belgium (in 1574) and was ultimately the heiress of the county of Wertheim, an immediate imperial fief, of which Ludwig became ruler by right of his wife in 1598.

Of Ludwig and Anne's four surviving sons, only the eldest, Christoph Ludwig (1568–1618), and Johann Dietrich (1585–1644) left descendants. Christoph Ludwig married Elisabeth von Manderscheid, heiress of Virneburg, and from 1621 his son took the title of Count of Loewenstein-Wertheim-Virneburg, while Johann Dietrich's heirs took the title of Count of Loewenstein-Wertheim-Rochefort. During the Thirty Years War, the Rochefort branch supported the Emperor and returned to the Catholic faith of their ancestors. The change of faith brought some advantage to the junior line and insured their elevation to the rank of Prince of the Holy Roman Empire in 1711, while the senior, Virneburg, line remained merely Counts. In 1559, with the extinction of the senior Palatinate line, the Loewensteins became the senior male line of the house of Wittelsbach. It was later argued that in the event of the extinction of the male line of both the Bavarian and Palatinate reigning house that these thrones should then pass to the Loewensteins.

In 1803 a series of French victories led to the Treaty of

Lunéville under which Virneburg and Rochefort were both ceded to France (although the family was compensated elsewhere). The family still retained their immediate County of Wertheim and so were formally included among the former sovereign houses of the Holy Roman Empire when it was finally dissolved in 1806. The King of Bavaria elevated the living males of the senior, Virneburg, branch to the rank of Prince (*Fürst*) on 19 November 1812, with the name Virneburg substituted by that of the newly acquired territory of Freudenberg. This title was then accorded by the King of Württemberg in a grant of 25 February 1813, and confirmed by the sovereigns of each of the other principal states in which the family held immediate territories (the Grand Duchy of Frankfurt in December 1812, the Grand Duchy of Hesse on 17 December 1812, the Grand Duchy of Würzburg on 24 January 1813 and the Grand Duchy of Baden on 3 April 1813).

The Congress of Vienna of 1815 decided that those former sovereign families which had owed direct allegiance to the Emperor should be accorded a special status, allowing them a form of equality with those families which after 1815 had retained their thrones. The German Confederation decided that those of princely rank would be accorded the style *Durchlaucht* (Most Serene Highness) and those of countly rank *Erlaucht* (Most Illustrious Highness) and both branches of the Loewenstein-Wertheim family were included in the former category. These 'mediatised' families were also authorised to establish or maintain their family 'house laws' which accorded the head of each family the right to authorise or refuse to accept as 'dynastic' the marriages of members of their families. However, in order for these house laws to have full legal validity they had to be registered in the parliaments of the states in which they held their rank and titles. Although the Freudenberg branch drew up strict laws requiring that members marry into countly families, they were never registered and so could not be legally enforced.*

The marriage of Johann Karl Ludwig, Count of Loewenstein-Wertheim-Freudenberg (1740–1816), in 1764 to Princess Dorothea Maria of Hesse-Philippsthal-Barchfeld, a branch of the family of the Grand Dukes and Electors of Hesse, may have influenced his elevation to the rank of Prince by the Bavarian King, especially since Johann's wife's mother was a Princess of Anhalt (of which family the Russian Empress Catherine the Great had been a member). Johann's younger brother Friedrich, who died in 1799, made the first 'unequal' marriage in the family and his two children instead took their mother's name and were given a modest financial settlement.†
Johann had twelve children but only two sons married and had descendants; the two wives of the elder, Georg, 2nd Prince of Loewenstein-Wertheim-Freudenberg (1775–1855) were both members of former sovereign houses, but Johann's younger son, Wilhelm (1783–1847), married a lady of more modest standing, albeit of old Prussian nobility, Dorothea von Kahlden, whose family provided numerous Prussian generals and senior officers. Georg's only surviving son Adolf (1805–61), married morganatically in 1831, to Catherine Schlundt (1807–77), who the Grand Duke of Baden created Baroness of Adlerhorst. Their elder son died young, leaving just one daughter, and eventually Adolf's father allowed

---

* The Rosenberg branch only required ancient nobility, an easier standard to meet and their laws were registered.
† This line became extinct with Friedrich's granddaughter in 1916.

Catherine to be accorded the rank of Erbfürstin von Loewenstein-Wertheim-Freudenberg, thus also extending princely rank to their daughter.

Adolf, who succeeded in 1855, died in 1861 aged just fifty-six, to be succeeded by his cousin Wilhelm (1817–87). Wilhelm's much younger brother, Leopold (1827–93), then serving as an officer in a Bavarian cavalry regiment and who like his uncle Adolf would convert to the Catholic faith, had fallen in love with Amalia Wollrabe (1836–1909). Adolf was still head of the house and willingly gave his consent to the marriage, which took place in the Evangelical Lutheran church of St Peter, in Hamburg, on 4 August 1861. Amalia, while not born to a noble family, was a member of a family of Hamburg patricians – Hamburg did not have a nobility, although the patriciate was similar to that of the early Renaissance Italian city-states.

Unfortunately Adolf died a few days after Leopold's marriage before his consent had been formalised, so the decision now reverted to Leopold's older brother Wilhelm, who was keen to restore his family's status after the embarrassment of his predecessor's wife's elevation as *Fürstin*. Wilhelm also wanted to retain the family's historic allegiance to the Protestant faith that both Adolf and Leopold had now abandoned. The advantage for the family of excluding descendants of such marriages was that they would no longer have any claim on the family 'fideicommis', or hereditary trusts, which were restricted to the descendants of 'equal' marriages. Leopold was initially able to get the support of the Bavarian King, Maximilian II, who was conscious that the two Loewenstein-Wertheim families were the senior legitimate branch of his own royal house. There remained some mystery about Amalia's true parentage and it has been proposed that she was really the daughter of Maximilian's father, the deposed King Ludwig I, renowned for his love of beautiful women and extramarital relationships.

When the liberally minded and tolerant Maximilian died at the early age of fifty-three, he was succeeded by his son the 'mad King' Ludwig II, then eighteen years old, who opposed the high nobility marrying outside their caste. Once former King Ludwig I had died in 1868, Leopold no longer had royal support. Wilhelm appealed to the new king who on 1 December 1869 conferred on Amalia the personal title of Baroness Wollrabe von Wallrab. Perhaps in acknowledgement of the circumstances of Amalia's birth, the king then granted her the more elevated title of Countess of Loewenstein-Scharffeneck in the Bavarian nobility, on 15 January 1875, with the same coat of arms as the first counts of Loewenstein-Wertheim. The choice of this name, the title of the senior branch of this family that had become extinct in 1633, may have been recognition that Amalia's status was more elevated than those other Loewenstein wives disqualified from taking their husband's rank.*

As the house laws remained unregistered there were no legal grounds for preventing Leopold's family from enjoying the princely titles, even if the king was unwilling to consent to their use at his own court. Nonetheless, Leopold's status and that of his wife was for some time undetermined; the *Almanach*

---

* An unusual footnote in the 1871 Almanach de Gotha refers to the uncertain circumstances of her birth; a surprising assertion bearing in mind her official birth records were never a matter of dispute. This note serves to support the belief that her parentage was more elevated than the official record suggested.

de Gotha records his religious conversion from the 1862 edition onwards without mention of his marriage, but then the 1868 and 1869 editions note that he had married 'morganatically', the latter word being dropped from the 1870 edition but without mention of his wife. Then, in 1871, Leopold is included along with the fact of his marriage to Amalia, with her title of Baroness Wollrabe von Wallrab, while the first four of their five children are listed in the *Almanach* as Princes and Princesses of Loewenstein-Wertheim-Freudenberg. All subsequent editions merely mention his marriage and the identity of his wife, without listing either their children or including the word 'morganatic'.

Leopold and Amalia had five children, two sons and three daughters, two of whom made religious profession while the eldest never married. Their elder son, Friedrich, died unmarried at the age of twenty-eight, leaving only their younger son, Maximilian, to marry and leave descendants. Maximilian was unwilling to accept what he considered an unjust humiliation over his title and quarrelled with his uncle Wilhelm. Faced with Wilhelm's intransigence, Maximilian insisted on his right to use the princely title, angering his uncle and making reconciliation even more difficult.

Although he was a difficult man Maximilian had great charm and intelligence: even while serving as an officer in the army, he translated Caesar's *Gallic Wars*, reflecting the quality of his classical education and that he shared the sophisticated tastes of Kings Ludwig I and Maximilian II. Maximilian's uncle Wilhelm died in 1887 but his son and heir, Ernst, married to a Prussian countess, was no less determined to resist his nephew's demands, particularly as to have done otherwise might have encouraged other morganatic descendants to demand similar treatment and perhaps a greater share of the family inheritance.

In 1895 Maximilian married a considerable heiress, the Hon. Constance Worms, whose father, Baron Henry de Worms (a grandson of Nathan Meyer Rothschild), had a few months earlier been created Lord Pirbright (the second Jew, after his cousin Lord Rothschild, to be created a British peer).* Constance's mother, Baroness Fanny von Todesco, was also from an ennobled Jewish family, with connections to many of the leading banking families of Europe. Henry de Worms had had a successful career in the law, as a barrister, and for fifteen years as a MP, serving as a junior minister in the government of Lord Salisbury and being appointed a privy councillor in 1888. Maximilian proved to be a less than devoted husband and he and Constance were divorced in 1912, having had two daughters and three sons; she wished to remarry and three years later Maximilian himself remarried, this time to a German noblewoman, Baroness Adelheid von Berlinchingen, but had no further children.

In 1919 a new German law converted all titles to names, requiring that everyone bearing a noble title adopt their father's title as part of their name; thus Maximilian's became Herr Maximilian Prinz von Loewenstein-Wertheim-Freudenberg, the title he had in any case legally inherited under the original patent, while also remaining Count of Loewenstein-Scharffeneck. Maximilian and Constance had

---

* Lord Pirbright (1840–1903) converted to the Anglican faith after his divorce from Fanny von Todesco, and is buried, with his second wife, in the church of St Mark's, Wyke. His splendid funeral monument, itself a Grade II listed building, includes mention of his children and grandchildren.

five children, two daughters and three sons; the eldest, Sophie, married Count Arbeno von Attems, of an ancient family long established in the border region between Austria and modern Italy and now part of the latter (her grandson is the present Lord Aylmer). The next daughter, Françoise, married an Austrian and moved to the United States before the Second World War. Maximilian's eldest son Johann, born in Munich, married twice but had no issue; the youngest, Hubertus, whose rank as a Prince of Loewenstein-Wertheim-Freudenberg was recognised by the then head of the house after the Second World War, died in 1984, leaving three daughters. Hubertus not only served in the German Bundestag but also played an important role in the Allied Denazification commission following the end of the Second World War.

Leopold (1903–74),* Maximilian's second son and Rupert's father, had no great inheritance and, soon after his marriage on 6 July 1932 to Bianca Fischler, Countess von Treuberg (1913–84), with the Nazis newly come to power, left Germany for Spain, where Rupert, their only son, was born in August 1933. Bianca Fischler was the daughter of Ernest Fischler, Count von Treuberg (1874–1950), a Bavarian royal chamberlain, and Henriette (Hette) von Kaufmann-Asser (1880–1944), whose grandfather, a leading banker, had in 1870 received the title of hereditary knight (*Ritter*) from the King of Prussia and whose father was an art collector and adviser to the German

---

* Whose memoir about his second wife, Diana, *A Time to Live, A Time to Die*, was published in 1970. He also translated into English Eduard Morike's amusing novella, *Mozart's Journey to Prague* (first published in German in 1856), Adelbert von Chamisso's Faustian tale, *Peter Schlemihl*, and Pastor Dietrich Bonhoeffer's study on *Ethics*, among other works.

finance minister. Henriette's brothers had distinguished careers: Heinrich (1882–1954) having served in the Foreign Office became German Ambassador to Argentina until his dismissal in September 1933, while Wilhelm (1888–1959) was a leading German film producer married to Henny Porten, one of the most renowned German screen actresses whose career survived the move from silent to speaking roles, until the film careers of both were boycotted when the Nazis came to power.

Hette herself was at the centre of a notable intellectual circle which included the composer Richard Strauss and painter Arnold Böcklin, but after the birth of their third child she and her husband divorced, largely because of her dedication to the pacifist movement. Her salon made her one of the most influential figures in contemporary German society with extraordinary social connections as well as ties with the highest level of government (and close friendship with the Bavarian Crown Prince Rupprecht). After the war her salon again became a magnet for leading intellectuals and politicians, until she fled rising anti-Semitism in Germany for exile in Switzerland. Her daughter Bianca, Rupert's mother, divorced Leopold in 1947 and remarried Peter Rosoff, whom she had met when he was posted to the US Embassy as a Colonel; Leopold also remarried, to Diana Gollancz, the daughter of the renowned publisher Sir Victor Gollancz.

The Line of Descent of the Princes zu Löwenstein-Wertheim-Freudenberg

Luitpold

Count in CARINTHIA, d. 907

m. Kunigunde, daughter of Berthold,
Count Palatine in SWABIA, d. 913

|

ARNULF

Duke of BAVARIA, d. 937

m. 910, Countess Judith von FRIAUL

|

Berthold

Margrave of NORDGAU,
d. 980

m. Countess Eila (Heilika)
von WALDECK, d. 1015

|

Henry

Margrave of the NORDGAU and
of SCHWEINFURT, d. 1017

m. Countess Gerberga, daughter of Count Otto

|

Henry

Count of the REGNITZ

m. Countess NN von ALTDORF

|

OTTO I

Count von SCHEYERN, d. 1072

m. 1057, Countess Haziga von DIESSEN,
d. 1104

|

OTTO II

Count von SCHEYERN, d. 1110

m. Countess Richardis von ORLAMÜNDE,
d. 1120

|

| WITTELSBACH |

|

OTTO IV

Count von WITTELSBACH,
Count Palatine of BAVARIA, d. 1156

m. Countess Heilika von PETTENDORF, d. 1170

|

OTTO (V) I

Duke of BAVARIA, d. 1183

m. 1157, Countess Agnes von LOOZ
and RIENECK, d. 1191

|

LOUIS I

Duke of BAVARIA, 1174–1231

m. 1204, Duchess Ludmilla of BOHEMIA,
d. 1240

OTTO II

Duke of BAVARIA and Count Palatine of
the RHINE, 1206–1253

m. 1227, Countess Agnes Palatine of
the RHINE, d. 1267

|

LOUIS II

Duke of UPPER BAVARIA, 1229–1294

m. (III) 1273, Countess Mathilda von HABSBURG,
d. 1304,
daughter of King RUDOLPH

|

RUDOLPH I

Duke of BAVARIA, Count Palatine of
the RHINE, 1274–1319

m. Royal Princess and Countess Mathilde
of NASSAU, d. 1323,
daughter of Adolf, German King

|

ADOLPH I

Duke of BAVARIA, 1300–1327

m. 1320, Countess Irmgard von ÖTTINGEN,
d. 1389

|

RUPERT II

Duke of BAVARIA, 1325–1398

m. 1345, Princess Beatrix of SICILY, d. 1365,
daughter of King Peter II

|

RUPERT III

GERMAN KING, 1352–1410

m. 1374, Countess Elizabeth von HOHENZOLLERN,
Burgravine of NÜRNBERG, 1353–1411

|

LOUIS III*

Duke of BAVARIA, 1378–1436

m. (II) 1417, Countess Mathilde of SAVOY, d. 1438

|

FREDERICK I

'The Victorious', Elector PALATINE, 1425–1476

m. 1471, Klara TOTT, d. 1520

|

Louis I of BAVARIA

Count von LÖWENSTEIN, Lord zu SCHARFENECK,
1463–1524

m. 1488 Elizabeth von MONTFORT, d. 1503

|

Frederick

Count von LÖWENSTEIN, Lord zu SCHARFENECK,
1502–1541

m. 1524, Helene von KÖNIGSEGG, 1509–1566

* see page 255

Louis III
Count von LÖWENSTEIN-WERTHEIM, 1530–1611
m. 1566, Countess Anna zu STOLBERG, 1531–1599,
heiress of WERTHEIM and ROCHEFORT

Christopher Louis
Count zu LÖWENSTEIN-WERTHEIM and VIRNEBURG,
1568–1618
m. 1592, Countess Elisabeth von MANDERSCHEID,
1569–1621, heiress of VIRNEBURG

Frederick Louis
Count zu LÖWENSTEIN-WERTHEIM and VIRNEBURG,
1598–1657
m. 1622, Countess Anna Hedwig zu STOLBERG,
1599–1634

Frederick Eberhard
Count zu LÖWENSTEIN-WERTHEIM-VIRNEBURG,
1629–1683
m. (II) 1681, Countess Susanna Sophie von
HOHENLOHE-WALDENBURG,
1648–1691

Henry Frederick
Count zu LÖWENSTEIN-WERTHEIM-VIRNEBURG,
1682–1721
m. 1703, Countess Amöne Sophie Friederike
zu LIMBURG, 1684–1746

Louis I of BAVARIA
Count von LÖWENSTEIN
John Louis Vollrath
Count zu LÖWENSTEIN-WERTHEIM-VIRNEBURG,
1705–1790
m. 1738, Countess Friederike Charlotte Wilhelmine
zu ERBACH-ERBACH,
1722–1786

JOHN CHARLES LOUIS
1st Prince (Fürst)
zu LÖWENSTEIN-WERTHEIM-FREUDENBERG,
1740–1816
m. 1764, Langravine Dorothea of
HESSE-PHILIPPSTHAL-BARCHFELD,
1738–1799

Prince (Prinz) William
zu LÖWENSTEIN-WERTHEIM-FREUDENBERG,
1783–1847
m. 1812, Dorothea Christine von KAHLDEN,
1791–1860

Prince (Prinz) Leopold
zu LÖWENSTEIN-WERTHEIM-FREUDENBERG,
1827–1893
m. 1861, Amalie WOLLRABE, created Baroness (Freifrau),
WOLLRABE von WALLRAB and Countess (Gräfin) von
LÖWENSTEIN-SCHARFFENECK, 1836–1909

Prince (Prinz) Maximilian
zu LÖWENSTEIN-WERTHEIM-FREUDENBERG,
Count von LÖWENSTEIN-SCHARFFENECK,
1871–1952
m. 1895, The Honourable Constance,
Baroness von WORMS,
1875–1963, daughter of Henry,
1st Baron PIRBRIGHT

Prince (Prinz) Leopold
zu LÖWENSTEIN-WERTHEIM-FREUDENBERG,
Count von LÖWENSTEIN-SCHARFFENECK,
1903–1974
m. 1932, Countess Bianca Henriette Maria
FISCHLER von TREUBERG, 1913–1984†

Prince (Prinz) Rupert
zu LÖWENSTEIN-WERTHEIM-FREUDENBERG
Count von LÖWENSTEIN-SCHARFFENECK, 1933-
m. 1957, Josephine Clare LOWRY-CORRY, 1931-
Daughter of Captain Montagu William LOWRY-CORRY of the
Earls BELMORE, by his wife The Honourable Mary Constance
BIDDULPH, daughter of 2nd Baron BIDDULH

Father Rudolf
zu LÖWENSTEIN-WERTHEIM-
FREUDENBERG OP,
1957–

The Rev Konrad
zu LÖWENSTEIN-WERTHEIM-
FREUDENBERG,
1958–

Princess Maria Theodora
zu LÖWENSTEIN-WERTHEIM-FREUDENBERG,
1966–
m. 1998 Count Manfredi della GHERARDESCA,
dei Conti di DONORATICO, di CASTAGNETO,
di BOLGHERI, di SETTIMO, di PIETRAROSSA,
dei Conti Palatino and of the Holy Roman Empire,
Patricians of Florence, of Pisa, of Voltera, Nobles of Sardinia

† see page 254

Count Aliotto
della GHERARDESCA, 2000–

Countess Margherita
della GHERARDESCA, 2002–

The Line of Descent of Countess Bianca Fischler von Treuberg

CHARLES V
Holy Roman Emperor, King of SPAIN,
1500–1558
m. 1526, Infanta Isabel of PORTUGAL,
1503–1539

PHILIP II
King of SPAIN, 1527–1598
m. (IV) 1570, Archduchess Anna of AUSTRIA,
1549–1580

HENRY IV
King of FRANCE and NAVARRE, 1553–1610
m. (II) 1600, Marie de'MEDICI, 1573–1666,
daughter of Francis, Grand Duke of TUSCANY

PHILIP III
King of SPAIN, 1578–1621
m. 1599, Archduchess Margaret of AUSTRA,
1584–1611

LOUIS XIII
King of FRANCE and NAVARRE, 1601–1643
m. 1615

Anna of AUSTRIA
Infanta of SPAIN, 1601–1666

LOUIS XIV
King of FRANCE and NAVARRE,
1638–1715
m. 1660, María Theresa of AUSTRIA,
Infanta of SPAIN, 1638–1683

DOM PEDRO I
Emperor and Perpetual Defender of BRAZIL,
1798–1834
by Domitilia de CASTRO do CANTO e MELLO,
created Viscountess de CASTRO
and Marchioness de SANTOS, 1797–1867

Louis
Le Grand Dauphin,
1661–1711
m. 1680, Princess Mary Anne of BAVARIA,
1660–1690

**Dona Isabel Maria de
Alcântara Brasileira, de BRAGANZA,**
recognised by her father, legitimated and created
Duchess de GOYAZ with the qualification of
Highness by Imperial Decree of 4th July 1826
1824–1898
m. 1843, Ernst Joseph Johann FISCHLER II
Count (Gräf) von TREUBERG
by his wife Countess (Gräfin)
of HOHENZOLLERN-SIGMARINGEN

PHILIP V
Duke of ANJOU, King of SPAIN and
the INDIES, 1683–1746
m. (II) 1714, Elizabeth FARNESE,
Princess of PARMA, 1692–1766

Ferdinand FISCHLER
III Count von TREUBERG,
1845–1897
m. 1873, Rosine Marie Theresia
von POSCHINGER, 1849–1897

CHARLES III
Duke of PARMA and PIACENZA (1731–1735)
King of NAPLES and SICILY (1735–1759)
King of SPAIN and the INDIES (1759–1788)
1716–1788
m. 1738, Princess Mary Amalia of SAXONY,
1724–1760

**Ernst Ludwig Ferdinand
Franz Xaver FISCHLER**
IV Count von TREUBERG, 1874–1950
m. 1904, Henriette Irmengard
von KAUFFMANN-ASSER, 1880–1944

CHARLES IV
King of SPAIN and the INDIES,
1747–1819
m. 1765, Princess Mary Louise of PARMA,
1751–1820

**Countess Bianca Henriette
Maria FISCHLER von TREUBERG,**
1913–1984

**Doña Carlota Joaquina
de BORBÓN y BORBÓN**
Infanta of Spain, 1775–1830
m. 1790, Dom JOÃO VI, King of PORTUGAL
and the ALGARVES, 1767–1826

The Line of Descent of Prince Rupert of the Rhine

Stephen*

Count Palatine of the RHINE, zu SIMMERN
and ZWEIBRÜCKEN, 1385–1459

m. 1410, Countess Anna von VELDENZ, d. 1439

|

Frederick I

Count Palatine of the RHINE, 1417–1480

m. 1454, Duchess Margaret von GELDERN, d. 1486

|

John I

Count Palatine of the RHINE, 1459–1509

m. 1481, Countess Johanna of NASSAU, 1464–1521

|

John II

Count Palatine of the RHINE, 1492–1557

m. 1508, Margravine Beatrix of BADEN, 1492–1534

|

FREDERICK III

Elector Palatine of the RHINE, 1515–1576

*m. 1537, Margravine Marie of
BRANDENBURG-KULMBACH, 1519–1567*

|

LOUIS VI

Elector Palatine of the RHINE, 1539–1583

m. 1560, Landgravine Elisabeth of HESSE, 1539–1582

|

FREDERICK IV

Elector Palatine of the RHINE, 1574–1610

*m. 1593, Countess Luise Juliane of NASSAU,
Princess of ORANGE, 1576–1644*

|

FREDERICK V

Elector Palatine of the RHINE,
King of BOHEMIA (1619–1621), 1596–1632

*m. 1613, Princess Elizabeth STUART, 1596–1662,
eldest daughter of King James VI
of SCOTLAND and I of ENGLAND,
by his Consort Queen Anne of DENMARK*

|

Rupert

Count Palatine of the RHINE,
Duke of BAVARIA, 1619–1682

*General of the Horse to his uncle King CHARLES I
in the Civil War, founder of the Royal Society.*

* Brother of LOUIS III, Duke of Bavaria

Key & Notes

d.　Died
m.　Married
NN　Name not known

Fürst indicates that the Prince is the head of the family – the other male Princes at the time would bear the title Prinz.

Names in capitals indicate that the person was head of their House.

WITTELSBACH

The House of WITTELSBACH was founded by OTTO IV, Count of WITTELSBACH (d. 1156), ranking second only to the Hapsburgs among the German Catholic dynasties of Europe.

Pages 252–3 show the line of descent from Luitpold, Count in Carinthia to Prince Rupert Loewenstein, and on to Prince Rupert's children and grandchildren. Page 254 shows the line of descent of Prince Rupert's mother, and page 255 the line of descent of his ancestral relation Prince Rupert of the Rhine, commander of the Royalist Cavalry during the English Civil War.

The achievement below represents the arms of the Princes zu Löwenstein-Wertheim-Freudenberg.

Genealogical research by Don Victor Franco de Baux.

Acknowledgements

Acknowledgments are due to the following people. Without their help, I would not have got this far:

My wife Josephine and my children, the Rev. Father Rudolf OP, the Rev. Konrad and Dora, who all supplied thoughtful comments and helpful ideas. I hope Konrad will feel he was successful in his worthwhile endeavours to have the book shorn of its more questionable comments.

I discussed the book with some of my great friends who have known me well over the last sixty years, especially John Bellingham, Michael Dormer and Lord Moyne.

Philip Dodd, for his encouragement and assistance in setting down these memories.

Guy Sainty and Don Victor Franco de Baux for their invaluable advice on the genealogy and ancestry of my family.

For their support and organisation: Dee Anstice, Jules Kopec, Pandora Millen, Jim Pfenninger and Sally Renny.

For their help in exploring the photographs in the family archive: Emily Hedges and Laurence Hill.

Gerrit te Spenke and Jan Favie, for their helpful comments.

Ian Shackleton at the Chatham Archive, Christopher Sykes and Alan Williams, for their assistance.

The publishing team at Bloomsbury, for their encouragement, especially Nigel Newton, Michael Fishwick and Anna Simpson.

Last, I must thank the Rolling Stones for the years we voyaged together through waters often uncharted, occasionally choppy, but always enthralling.

Index of Names

A Note on the Author

Born in Palma, Majorca in 1933, Prince Rupert Loewenstein lived in London and Paris, and studied medieval history at Oxford before becoming a stockbroker for the American firm Bache & Co. In 1963 he formed a consortium that bought the merchant bank Leopold Joseph & Sons. Five years later he met Mick Jagger and managed the Rolling Stones' finances until 2008. Prince Rupert lives in Petersham, near Richmond, with his wife Princess Josephine; they have three children.

A Note on the Type

The text of this book is set in Adobe Caslon, named after the English punch-cutter and type-founder William Caslon I (1692–1766). Caslon's rather old-fashioned types were modelled on seventeenth-century Dutch designs, but found wide acceptance throughout the English-speaking world for much of the eighteenth century until being replaced by newer types towards the end of the century. Used in 1776 to print the Declaration of Independence, they were revived in the nineteenth century, and have been popular ever since, particularly amongst fine printers. There are several digital versions, of which Carol Twombly's Adobe Caslon is one.